PARK
WALKING
IN
SAN DIEGO
COUNTY

Park Walking in San Diego County

by
William Carroll

First Edition

Printed in the United States of America
ISBN 0-910390-32-0
Library of Congress Catalog Card Number: 91-73240

Coda Publications
P.O. Bin 711
San Marcos, California 92079-0711

For those many fine people who overcome
so many obstacles in the creation
and maintenance of our public parks.

Contents

"We all grow older but we do not have to become old"

The Singles' Philosopher

Park Walking in San Diego County

There are over 380 public parks in San Diego County, the majority of which have walking space for everyone with time to enjoy better health or relax in the midst of picnic and playground facilities for the most aggressive family.

Southern California's mild climate succeeds in making the use of public parks a year-around delight and outdoor recreation a pleasant routine. Both could make the difference between leading a sedentary existence or living with buoyant energy that has been untapped since the last time you enjoyed a relaxing day in natural surroundings.

Park Walking in San Diego County reveals hundreds of possible walks in and around the area's inland public parks. In this book park walks range from peaceful strolls to miles-long ventures through some of the nation's finest public land. Park acreage has been listed where known except for a few small "mini-parks" which occupy only a tiny portion of a city block. These are so noted. Beach-front parks and recreation facilities are detailed in the companion volume *Beach Walking in San Diego County*. Urban mall walking is covered by *Mall Walking in San Diego County* which is the first book of this series.

Park description pages are sequenced by name of the city or community area in which the park is located. The sub-listing is by the common name of the park. Each listing includes the park's address and city location. Those parks without a parking lot are identified by a reference to "street" parking. *The Thomas Guide* of street maps for San Diego and Imperial County is used to provide each park's specific page and grid location on street maps of the area. In addition, there are references to sources of public transportation and schedule information. Many parks located midway between the City of San Diego and what is termed North County are blessed with two public transportation systems: One from the south, another from the north.

No site maps or measured walks are included with *Park Walking in San Diego County* as pathways change from year to year. An inexpensive pedometer attached to your belt could provide distance information as you explore the many parks. Reference material on each page provides a general description of facilities available and lists typical open hours. In some instances park open hours change from season to season and a telephone call is recommended before driving any great distance. Additional notations define the availability of public rest rooms, benches and picnic facilities inside the park boundaries. Photographs with many listings usually show the entry drive as seen by a motorist which makes it easy to find the inside parking lot if one is available.

Final pages of *Park Walking in San Diego County* contain a cross-index to find a walking site by the common name of the park and be directed to it's page number. The reverse index listing is by city or community area from which you can find the name and page number of parks in that locale.

The complete list includes: Federal Parks, State of California Parks, County of San Diego Parks, a wide variety of City Parks and a few Special District Parks. Accordingly, these listed walking sites vary from the largest urban park in the nation to tiny neighborhood "mini-parks" with little more than playground equipment and sand-boxes. Many of the medium-size parks offer enchanting opportunities for neighborhood walks. Parks in the City of El Centro, in Imperial County, have been listed for readers who would like to combine viewing the spectacular Borrego Desert with a distant park-walking excursion. Adjoining San Diego County on the north is Riverside County's "Old West" theme town of Temecula which has its three city parks listed.

Visitors to area parks will often find that restroom facilities are mapped on a Directory Board located near the main entrance or arrowed on a Ranger Station wall. Public telephones may be in the same area. Many parks provide printed folders showing walking trails and picnic areas. Others rely on sign-posting to direct walkers along maintained pathways.

Park walking is totally different from hiking or backpacking. The latter two recreations often involve natural trails that are not maintained, include steep climbs and lead through remote areas. On the other hand, park walking is usually through maintained natural surroundings on well-used pathways and seldom in remote areas of the County. In some rural parks, Rangers staff the facility on a round-the-clock basis. Urban and suburban parks will often be surrounded by a shopping or residential complex concealed behind a screen of trees or shrubs.

Food is a modest problem while park walking because it is a rare park that has a snack stand. On the other hand it is a rewarding experience to pack a picnic lunch, drive to a park and walk for pleasure. When it's time to rest, the picnic lunch can provide all that is needed in the way of refreshment and replacement of pounds lost by exercise walking. Most San Diego parks have picnic tables and over half provide barbecue grills.

Within *Park Walking in San Diego County* you will discover many new walking sites worth visiting. This book's specific information on how to get there, what you will find on arrival, and suggestions for walks will make it easy to exercise with confidence and pleasure.

Walking and Health

Most of us find it hard to argue against such good old-fashion values as motherhood, apple pie and better health. Or disagree with millions of people who enjoy the natural surroundings of public parks as the site of their personal walking venture.

Park walking techniques are simple, the cost low and opportunities everywhere for healthful recreational exercise. Most parks in the inland area of San Diego County are suitable for such use and many are within easy reach by public transportation. However food services are not usually available. This should not be be considered a valid excuse to ignore regular walking ventures as an aid to creating a more fruitful lifestyle.

A good level of health-supporting activity is said to be about 30 minutes of moderately fast walking four times a week. Should you be overweight, walk for a longer period of time and eat less until the weight problem is minimal and your body chemistry becomes balanced. Medical reports indicate that a body in good condition does a better job of using its food intake than does a body in poor condition. This is considered to be another way of saying that a healthy body gains less from the same meal that would add unwanted pounds onto a body less functional.

It was also reported that about three months of consistent vigorous exercise will bring almost any useful body up to its reasonable peak. Many health enthusiasts work out in a gym or spa to build muscles, jog or run and gain wind, or lift weights to enhance what they are able to raise off the ground. Generally speaking these are add-ons to being in good physical condition. In the beginning; the values of feeling better and being more in control are the initial, and the most important, benefits of simply walking your way to better health.

It is worth pointing out that when you plan any walking venture to be a vigorous workout, begin with five or ten minutes of slow walking to give the body time to warm up to its new task. Once warmed up, consider walking a mile in about 15 minutes. This equals four miles an hour which is a fairly rapid pace over the ups and downs of park pathways. The secret to making this a maximum-effort walk is a full swing of the arms with every step. In effect this adds upper body exercise to benefits usually reserved for legs, lungs and heart. The arm-waving technique should be practiced for short distances over a period of several walking ventures while building up to its use for a full mile. You may meet walkers who have added one or two weights to their wrists, or carry plastic containers of water in each hand, as additions to the workout factor. It is estimated they gain four or five percent more benefit from their workout by adding such weight. A similar advantage could be achieved by walking five percent further and leaving the accessories at home.

When possible, arrange to walk with a partner or group. Comparisons and challenges add pleasure to the venture because friends will often cause you to exercise a bit harder than you might push by yourself. All of which adds up to a greater measure of improvement to overall health.

As you walk with others you will notice as many postures as there are walkers. How you upgrade your body could begin with standing comfortably erect to raise the rib cage and give your lungs the maximum amount of space within which to expand. Then maintain your shoulders back and level by noting where the thumbs touch your thighs. Unless your arms are grossly unequal, the thumbs should be in about the same place on each side. A further improvement in posture will come from pulling your stomach in and thrusting the hip joints forward to set the spine in a near vertical position. This tends to eliminate the "swayback" posture which causes so many complaints of aching back.

Swing your arms naturally and use a normal length step while warming up. After the five minute warm-up, begin swinging your legs forward and striding out as far as is comfortable. This striding-out technique exercises muscles with a bit of gentle stretching. It also allows the hip joints a chance to explore new territory and reduce their aches and pains from the stiffness of inaction. Move each foot well out, put it down on the heel, roll the foot forward and pick up cleanly. Practice an aggressive walking technique with the same attention you would give the game of golf. Then, when postured walking becomes so natural you no longer think about it, take a good look at yourself in a store window as you stroll past. The new image of a healthy well-figured person will be all the reward you will need.

There appears to be very little difference between health benefits from exercise walking as compared to operating a treadmill or stair-step device. It simply boils down to how long you walk, whether uphill or down, and slow or fast: Plus how convenient it is to exercise when and where.

Shoe selection for walking lends itself to more questions than ordering dinner in a foreign country where one does not speak the language. The most important factor of a well-fitting shoe is that it be comfortable to the entire foot. Secondly, buy only a shoe designed for walking; which running, jogging, tennis, mountain climbing and basketball shoes are not.

A top-quality shoe similar to that shown on the next page will be less expensive in the long run and provide maximum support for your hard-working feet. There's little problem finding the proper last for it is said there are over 200 different models available. Some manufacturers produce men's and women's walking shoes with widths from AAAA to EE, in sizes 4 to 14. Once past the size problem, look for a shoe with dark-colored fabric uppers (which appear clean longer) that breathe easily and allow your feet to perspire without drowning. For park walking you need a moderately firm outer sole and a cushioned inner sole to protect delicate foot bones from the continual impact of the great variety of surfaces found in public parks. Surfaces may range from asphalt, smooth dirt, decomposed granite, gravel, small rocks and rain-washed hard clay. The outer sole should be sufficiently firm to protect the foot from unexpected pressure points of rocks or sharp sticks. Wide deep grooves in the sole are essential for good traction on gravel or loose dirt and sand. If you have a tendency to wear a shoe's sole off to either side, purchase ankle-high tops to support your ankles and straighten your walk.

Typical high-tech walking shoes have features similar to this New Balance model which demonstrates advanced technology to promote walking efficiency.

Leather tongue and quarter lining provide a comfortable wearing surface.

A firm saddle area is important for mid-foot support.

Soft leather uppers present a fine appearance and many are perforated for breathability. Man-made fabrics may dry more rapidly and pass additional cooling air.

A modern inside vamp lining wicks moisture from the foot.

The midsole must be firm to maintain stability yet be flexible to make walking easy. Multi-density midsoles often have a soft heel pad for cushioning and a firm arch area to efficiently translate the walker's body-weight to the forefoot.

The molded counter portion of the footbed rolls upward at the sides and rear to keep the foot in place. An extended reinforcement maintains structural integrity of the shoe while stabilizing the mid- and rear-foot area.

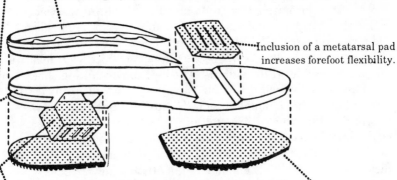

Inclusion of a metatarsal pad increases forefoot flexibility.

A heel insert assists in forward-motion transfer of leg and body-weight from the point of heel strike to lift off for the next step.

An abrasion-resisting outsole should be of semi-hard material with ridging, or lug-pattern tread design, for good traction. Dual-density outsoles can provide protection from sharp objects and additional cushioning for the feet.

It is worth keeping in mind that while high shoes offer better support, they are heavier; about which more later. Low shoes may be easier to walk in but provide the least support. It is worth considering the type of park in which you plan to do most of the walking. The more natural, or undeveloped, the park the more desirable the hightop for maximum protection from the abrasion potential of protruding rocks or sharp branches. A low shoe would work very well in a mid-city park with fully maintained or paved pathways from which all shrubs have been trimmed back. A good compromise is the well-designed walking shoe with a collar which fits snugly below the ankle and is sufficiently flexible to be comfortable.

For sure; bring or buy a pair of thick walking socks to wear while trying on new shoes: Otherwise you could end up with shoes that will be much too tight when put to hard use. Begin with making sure the shape of the sole matches your foot then, when standing in the laced shoe, insist on from 1/3rd to 1/2-inch of space between your big toe and end of the shoe. If the area over the toe is high, and there is plenty of room between your toenail and interior of the shoe, that is a plus. A padded roll around the top with an extension pad up the back, which is called a scree collar, can be good or bad depending on fit of the shoe and what feels most comfortable to you. A well-fitting upper must lace to a snug fit around the entire foot to keep it from sliding inside the shoe and wearing blisters as you walk.

An informative test could be a fast and hard walk-about inside the store in the shoes you are planning to buy. This is a good way to be reasonably sure their areas of flexibility and stiffness are harmonious with the manner in which your feet are most comfortable while walking. The best park-walking shoes will have a sole which is flexible enough to bend naturally forward from the moment you plant your heel until you move forward and lift the toe area to take another step. Poor shoes could quickly become painful and inhibit your pleasure.

Two final points to consider: One is shoe weight. You will pick them up and lay them down many thousands of times during a day's walk. The less they weigh the easier walking is. On the other hand a heavy shoe gives your muscles more of a workout. Leather walkers usually weigh more than shoes made with uppers of man-made breathable fabrics and should be well broken in before going on a long hard walk.

Park Walking in San Diego County

The second point is flexibility. A soft shoe that is too flexible provides little assistance to control your stride. A stiff shoe provides extra stride control but may feel like a Dutch wooden clog. Try for a comfortable balance between soft and firm, with a bit of bias toward more firm than less, that makes you feel most secure while walking over a variety of surfaces.

Walking through parks during most Southern California seasons calls for the least possible investment in clothing. Underwear is best when made from polyester or polypropylene. These artificial fabrics allow natural body moisture to pass through and evaporate which helps keep your body at its normal temperature. Cotton is comfortable but tends to hold moisture and become soggy. Outerwear could be a simple sweat suit to keep you as warm as you like or loose fitting tropical clothing if you enjoy being a bit on the cool side. A light jacket would be a colorful identifier and enough protection for a final walk to the parking lot after you're finished. However, if you have to wait outside in the cold for public transportation, be sure to have an insulated outer jacket and head covering to keep from chilling. The hat can be worn and the jacket carried while walking.

During inclement weather, the more closely you maintain a normal body temperature the better your walk will be. Wear good quality thermal underwear made of an artificial fabric to pass and evaporate body moisture. Pants, shirts and sweaters should maintain warmth and be worn in layers as the temperature dictates. A good jacket with a weatherproof nylon outer surface over its inside lining of fleece or wool is desirable. You will find a headcovering welcome on a rainy day, during one of Southern California's infrequent wind storms, or when the sun is skin-burning hot. Double socks, thin pair inside, thick outside, do a good job or preventing blisters. In short, be comfortable.

Eating is seldom a bad idea and current opinions suggest that four light meals a day are best of all. Plan ahead to maintain your energy at a useful level instead of fighting the highs and lows associated with heavy spread-out meals. A light breakfast when you walk early will allow brunching at ten or eleven. Or brunch first, then walk the noon hours away. Break longer walks with a tea or lemonade stop, to rest the body and replace lost fluids. Carrying a walker's bottle of fluid from your belt loop is easy and most sports stores have a wide selection of bottles to choose from. If you snack while exercising select

Park Walking in San Diego County

carbohydrates and leave fatty, protein-rich, meals for social events and appreciation of mother's home cooking. One bit of good diet news which surfaced from a recent research project was a report indicating that mild exercise, like walking, greatly improved the body's beneficial use of protein. In effect, with regular exercise you may be able to enjoy a greater variety of tasty foods with less damage to your vitality.

According to the *Wellness Letter*, published by the University of California in Berkeley, being continually active is the key to weight control and good health for an average person. Burning 1000 calories a week in moderate activity is the *Letter's* basic recommendation for health-giving exercise. Normal health being considered, age appears to be of little importance. Reasonable activity has been shown to improve mobility and strength for individuals 80 and 90 years of age. Neck stiffness, back pain and headaches have long been known to become less a problem during and following regular exercise programs. A reduction of stress and improved cardio-vascular performance are believed to be responsible for the decrease in such painful common problems.

Not to mention that regular exercise has long been known to help us all live better and enjoy more.

Which is what walking is all about: Living better. No matter where you are in San Diego County, a nearby park is open to accommodate you. It's even possible that a bit of regular exercise would feel so great that a pleasant schedule of walking each week may be easy to establish. From then on it's all for the good: Fewer problems with weight control, better general health, and more new friends with similar objectives.

Walking for health is today's way to go.

How Each Walking Site Is Described

Location

Description: Size and what recreation facilities are available.
Located at: Street address or intersections, community name.
Transit service: The transportation district, bus number(s) and
      information telephone number.
Thomas Guide: Page, Grid. Where you will find this park site in
      the *Thomas Guide* of San Diego/Imperial County maps.
Open hours: When the park is open for public use. A few distant
      parks have winter/summer hours. Telephone ahead.
Jurisdiction: The government entity in control of the park and a
      telephone number for additional park information.
Restrooms, picnic tables and BBQs are listed when known.
Public telephone: Availability of a telephone for outgoing calls.
Walks: A brief description of parkways suitable for exercise
      walking and usefulness of the surrounding area. Many
      parksites are undergoing continual improvement and
      new parkways may often be found and enjoyed.

"Not feasible" indicates that exercise walking could be difficult
      or impossible due to terrain or unique conditions. A few
      such areas could be great fun for experienced hikers,
      backpackers or caravan campers.

"Not recommended" indicates the park is in an industrial or
      commercial area, surrounded by streets carrying a high
      volume of traffic or with a related problem where
      walking may be hazardous.

When using park driveways for walking, it is advisable to face
      oncoming traffic for maximum safety.

Allied Gardens

Allied Gardens Park

Description: Community pool, gym, ball court, play fields, totlot.
Located at 5155 Greenbriar Avenue, San Diego
Transit service: SDT #13, #115   Schedules: 233-3004
Thomas Guide: Page 54, Grid D/4   On site parking
Open: 24 Hours   Jurisdiction: City of San Diego   583-4450
Restrooms: Yes   Picnic tables: Yes   Public telephone: No
Walks: Parkway and nearby residential areas are useful.

Allied Gardens

Rancho Mission Canyon Park

Description: Picturesque slopes with playfields and totlot.
Located at 6005 Larchwood Avenue, San Diego
Transit service: No
Thomas Guide: Page 54, Grid E/3   On-site parking
Open: 24-Hours   Jurisdiction: City of San Diego   236-6661
Restrooms: No   Picnic tables/BBQs   Public telephone: No
Walks: Parkways, area residential and adjoining canyon
hillsides. A nice location for exercise walking.

Anza-Borrego

Agua Caliente Springs Park

Description: Hot springs, shaded camp sites amid 800 acres.
Located at 39555 County Highway S-2, Julian
Transit service: CTS #884   Schedules: 233-3004
Thomas Guide: Page 406, Grid C/4   On-site parking
Open: All year. Entry fee $1   County of San Diego   595-3600
Restrooms: Yes   Picnic tables/BBQs   Public telephone: Yes
Walks: There are many fine hiking trails in this unique park.

Park Walking in San Diego County

Anza-Borrego

Vallecito County Park

Description: Stage station site and camping, desert scenery.
Located at 37349 Highway S-2, Julian
Transit service: CTS #884   Schedules: 233-3004
Thomas Guide: Page 406, Grid C/4   On-site parking
Open: Sept to May   Jurisdiction: County of San Diego
Information: 694-3049   Restrooms: Yes   Picnic area: Yes
Telephone: Yes   Walks: Many desert hiking trails in the area.

Barrett Junction

Barrett Lake

Description: A water storage facility not open for hiking.
Located on Barrett Lake Road, off Highway 94, Dulzura
Transit service: No
Thomas Guide: Page 408, Grid C/5   Street parking
Open: Not open   Jurisdiction: City of San Diego
Information: 465-3474   Walks: No

Bay Park

Tecolate Canyon Natural Park

Description: Natural state 900-acre canyon area with a number
of ball fields at this entrance. Inquire for other entries.
Located at 4675 Tecolate Road, San Diego
Transit service: SDT # 5/105   Schedules: 233-3004
Thomas Guide: Page 59, Grid F/1   On-site parking
Open: 24 Hours   Jurisdiction: County of San Diego   490-0930
Restrooms: Yes   Picnic tables: Yes   Public telephone: No
Walks: There are miles of hiking trails in this superb park.

Bay Park   Tecolate Community Park

Description: Playing fields, ball court, baseball, golf, hiking, totlot and modern recreation center close to a residential area.
Located at 4675 Tecolate Road, San Diego
Transit service: SDT #5/105   Schedules: 233-3004
Thomas Guide: Page 59, Grid F/1   On-site parking
Open: 24 Hours   Jurisdiction: City of San Diego   236-6661
Restrooms: Yes   Picnic tables/BBQs   Public telephone: Yes
Walks: Parkways and miles Tecolate Canyon natural trails.

Bay Park   Western Hills Park

Description: Neighborhood park with playground and ball court.
Located at 4810 Kane Street, San Diego
Transit service: SDT #5/105   Schedules: 233-3004
Thomas Guide: Page 52, Grid F/5   On-site parking
Open: 24 Hours   Jurisdiction: City of San Diego   236-6661
Restrooms: No   Picnic tables/BBQs   Public telephone: No
Walks: Parkways, loop natural trail and nearby residential area.

Bonita   Sweetwater Heights Park

Description: Playground site near Plaza Bonita Shopping Mall
Located on Stockman Street at Sweetwater Road, National City
Transit service: NCT #601, #602, #604   Schedules: 233-3004
Thomas Guide: Page 69, Grid E/2
Open: 0800 to 2100 Jurisdiction: City of National City 336-4290
Restrooms: No   Picnic tables: Yes   Public telephone: No
Walks: Parksite, area roadways and in the Plaza Bonita Mall.

Bonita   Sweetwater Regional Park

Description: Undeveloped natural area, hiking/equestrian use.
Located at 3051 Equitation Lane, National City
Transit service: CVT #705   Schedules: 233-3004
Thomas Guide: Page 69 Grid F/2   On-site parking
Open: Dawn to dusk Jurisdiction: County of San Diego 490-0930
Information: 475-3134   Restrooms: Yes   Picnic area: No
Public telephone: Yes   Walks: On hiking and horse trails.

Borrego Springs

Description: The largest State Park in the United States.
Located at the end of Palm Canyon Drive, Borrego Springs
Transit service: No   Not suitable for walks in summer heat.
Thomas Guide: Page 402, Grid D/4   On-site parking
Open: Dawn to dusk   Jurisdiction: State of California   767-5311
Restrooms: Yes   Picnic tables: Yes   Public telephone: Yes
Walks: Obtain a park map for the 500 miles of primitive roads,
many hiking areas and in-park sites worthy of exploration.

Bostonia

Albert Van Zanten Park

Description: Play field, ball court, on parkland adjoining school.
Located at 1495 Greenfield Drive, El Cajon
Transit service: SDT #15   Schedules: 233-3004
Thomas Guide: Page 56, Grid E/2   Street parking
Open: 0700 to 2200   Jurisdiction: City of El Cajon   441-1754
Restrooms: No   Picnic area: No   Public telephone: No
Walks: Single long parkway and the nearby residential area.

Bostonia

Bostonia Park

Description: Recreation center, gym, ball courts, fields, totlot.
Located at 1049 Bostonia Street, El Cajon
Transit service: CTS #848, #864   Schedules: 233-3004
Thomas Guide: Page 56, Grid E/3   On-site parking
Open: 0700 to 2200   Jurisdiction: City of El Cajon   441-1670
Restrooms: Yes   Picnic tables: Yes   Public telephone: No
Walks: Loop paved parkway and in the nearby residential area.

Cardiff-By-The-Sea   Cardiff Park

Description: About 12 shaded acres with totlot. Adjoins school.
Located at San Elijo Avenue and Mozart Avenue, Cardiff
Transit service: NCTD #361   Schedules: 722 or 743-6283
Thomas Guide: Page 29, Grid B/1   Street parking
Open: Non-school hours.   Info: City of Encinitas 944-5080
Restrooms: No   Picnic tables: No   Public telephone: No
Walks: Paved parkway only. Area streets not suitable due to
heavy traffic and lack of sidewalks.

Carlsbad   Calaveras Park

Description: Recreation facility, gymnasium, totlot, baseball,
tennis, ballcourt, recreation equipment, on a 21-acre site.
Located at 2997 Glasgow Drive, Carlsbad
Transit service: NCTD #322   Schedules: 722- or 743-6283
Thomas Guide: Page 14, Grid D/3   On site parking
Open 24 Hours   Jurisdiction: City of Carlsbad   434-2923
Restrooms: Yes   Picnic tables/BBQs   Public telephone: Yes
Walks: Surrounding residential area is best at this busy park.

Carlsbad   Chase Field

Description: A baseball field complex with heavy use.
Located at 3400 Harding Street, Carlsbad
Transit service: NCTD #322   Schedules: 722 or 743-6283
Thomas Guide: Page 13, Grid F/4   Street parking
Open: 24 Hours   Jurisdiction: City of Carlsbad   434-2824
Restrooms: Yes   Picnic area: No   Public telephone: No
Walks: The surrounding residential area would be best.

Carlsbad   Heritage Hall/Magee Park

Description: Small downtown park with historic buildings and
public meeting room on a nicely shaded five-acre site.
Located at 258 Beech Avenue, Carlsbad
Transit service: NCTD # 301, # 321, # 322 Info 722- or 743-6283
Thomas Guide: Page 13, Grid E/4   On-site parking
Open: 24Hours   Jurisdiction: City of Carlsbad   434-2824
Restrooms: Yes   Picnic tables/BBQs   Public telephone: No
Walks: The best walks will be made in the adjoining area.

Carlsbad   Holiday Park

Description: Six-acres, totlot, ball court, shuffleb'rd, horseshoes.
Located on Pio Pico Drive at Chestnut Avenue, Carlsbad
Transit service: NCTD #321, #322   Schedules: 722- or 743-6283
Thomas Guide: Page 13, Grid F/4   Street parking
Open: 24 Hours   Jurisdiction: City of Carlsbad   434-2824
Restrooms: Yes   Picnic tables/BBQs   Public telephone: No
Walking: Open parkland and residential area recommended.

Carlsbad   Laguna Riviera Park

Description: Two-acre park, tennis, horseshoes and totlot.
Located at Kelly Drive and Park Drive, Carlsbad
Transit service: No
Thomas Guide: Page 14, Grid C/5   Street parking
Open: 24 Hours   Jurisdiction: City of Carlsbad   434-2824
Restrooms: Yes   Picnic area: Yes   Public Telephone: No
Walks: Adjacent area offers the best opportunities for exercise.

Carlsbad   Levante Park

Description: Baseball, ball courts and recreation/meeting room.
Located at 3025 Levante Street, Carlsbad
Transit service: NCTD # 304, # 309 Schedules: 722- or 743-6283
Thomas Guide: Page 25, Grid C/1   Street parking
Open: 24 Hours   Jurisdiction: City of Carlsbad   434-2824
Restrooms: Yes   Picnic area: No   Public Telephone: No
Walks: The upscale residential area offers the best walking.

Carlsbad   **Maxton Brown Park (Laguna State Park)**

Description: A tiny jewel of a park for reading and bird watching
over adjoining Buena Vista Lagoon.
Located at 500 Laguna Drive, Carlsbad
Transit service: NCTD # 301,# 321,# 322   Info: 722- or 743-6283
Thomas Guide: Page 13, Grid E/3   Scarce street parking
Open: 24 Hours   Jurisdiction: City of Carlsbad   434-2824
Restrooms: No   Picnic tables: Yes   Public telephone: No
Walks: The park is too small, the area not feasible, for walks.

Carlsbad   **Pine Field**

Description: Major use is for baseball.
Located at 3500 Harding Street, Carlsbad
Transit service: NCTD #322   Schedules: 722 or 743-6283
Thomas Guide: Page 13, Grid F/4   On-site parking
Open: 24 Hours   Jurisdiction: City of Carlsbad   434-2836
Restrooms: Yes   Picnic area: No   Public telephone No
Walks: Exercise walking would be best in the surrounding area.

Carlsbad   **Stagecoach Park**

Description: A fine community park on 28 acres with playing
fields, gymnasium, totlot and impressive landscaping.
Located at 3420 Camino de Los Coches, Carlsbad
Transit service: NCTD # 304   Schedules: 722- 743-6283
Thomas Guide: Page 25, Grid D/1   On-site parking
Open: 24 Hours   Jurisdiction: City of Carlsbad   434-2895
Restrooms: Yes   Picnic tables: Yes   Public telephone: Yes
Walking: Short paved parkways and nearby residential area.

Casa de Oro   **Avocado County Park**

Description: Seven acres of turf for passive recreation.
Located at 10925 Fury Lane, Spring Valley
Transit service: No
Thomas Guide: Page 63, Grid C/3   Street parking
Open: 24 Hours   Jurisdiction: County of San Diego   694-3049
Restrooms: No   Picnic area: No   Public Telephone: No
Walks: Grassed parksite only. Limited sidewalks in nearby area.

Casa de Oro   **Estrella County Park**

Description: An undeveloped County Park site.
Located at 9810 Sierra Madre Road, Spring Valley
Transit service: No
Thomas Guide: Page 63, Grid A/3   Street parking
Open: Not for public use   Jurisdiction: County of San Diego
Information: 694-3049   Restrooms: No   Picnic area: No
Public telephone: No   Walks:Site unsuitable. No area sidewalks.

Castle Park   **Lauderbach Park**

Description: Recreation center with totlot, ball court, play fields.
Located at 333 Oxford Street, Chula Vista
Transit service: SDT #39   Schedules: 233-3004
Thomas Guide: Page 71, Grid E/1   On-site parking
Open: 0800 to 2230   Jurisdiction: City of Chula Vista   691-5071
Restrooms: Yes   Picnic tables/BBQs   Public telephone: No
Walks: Not recommended. No parkways and heavy street traffic.

Castle Park   Sunbow Park

Description: A pleasant four acres with a playground, tennis,
play area, ball fields, an exercise trail and mature shade trees.
Located at 500 East Naples Street, Chula Vista
Transit service: CVT #703   Schedules: 233-3004
Thomas Guide: Page 70, Grid A/6   Street parking
Open: 0700 to 2230   Jurisdiction: City of Chula Vista   691-5071
Restrooms: No   Picnic area: No   Public telephone: No
Walks: The exercise path is recommended at your own pace.

Chollas Creek   Gompers Park

Description: Neighborhood park with shade trees and totlot.
Located at 4926 Hilltop Drive, San Diego
Transit service: SDT #5/105, #13, #16   Schedules: 233-3004
Thomas Guide: Page 66, Grid C/1   Street parking
Open: 24 Hours   Jurisdiction: City of San Diego   236-6661
Restrooms: Yes   Picnic tables/BBQs   Public telephone: No
Walks: There are a few parkways and the residential area.

Chollas Creek   Mid-City Athletic Area

Description: Baseball facilities known as Berardini Field.
Located at 4402 Federal Boulevard, San Diego
Transit service: No
Thomas Guide: Page 61, Grid C/6   On-site parking
Open: 24 Hours   Jurisdiction: City of San Diego   236-6661
Restrooms: No   Picnic area: No   Public telephone: No
Walks: Neither the baseball fields or area are suitable.

Chula Vista   Bay Boulevard Park

Description: Small neighborhood park with nice picnic area.
Located at Bay Boulevard and "F" Street, Chula Vista
Transit service: CVT #705, #707   Schedules: 233-3004
Thomas Guide: Page 69, Grid C/4   Street parking
Open: 0700 to 2230   Jurisdiction: City of Chula Vista   691-5071
Restrooms: No   Picnic area: Yes   Public telephone: No
Walks: The adjoining area is recommended for exercise walking.

Chula Vista

Discovery Park

Description: Nice community park with baseball fields, ball courts, PAR course, play fields and playground on a 15-acre site.
Located at 400 Buena Vista, Chula Vista
Transit service: CVT # 704   Schedules: 233-3004
Thomas Guide: Page 70, Grid E/4   Street parking
Open: 0700 to 2230   Jurisdiction: City of Chula Vista   691-5071
Restrooms: Yes   Picnic tables: Yes   Public telephone: No
Walks: There are paved parkways and a nearby residential area

Chula Vista

Eucalyptus Park

Description: A 20-acre shaded community park with ball fields, tennis, ball courts, playground and well-equipped totlot.
Located at 20 Fourth Avenue, Chula Vista
Transit service: CVT #706/706A, SDT #29   Schedules: 233-3004
Thomas Guide: Page 69, Grid C/3   On-site parking
Open: 0700 to 2230   Jurisdiction: City of Chula Vista   691-5071
Restrooms: Yes   Picnic tables/BBQs   Public telephone: No
Walks: There are few parkways. Area sidewalks recommended.

Chula Vista

Fred H. Rohr Park

Description: 63 Acres, equestrian park, playfields and totlot.
Located at 4370 and 4548 Sweetwater Road, Chula Vista
Transit service: CVT #705   Schedules: 233-3004
Thomas Guide: Page 70, Grid C/1   On-site parking
Open: 0900 to 2230   Jurisdiction: Chula Vista   691-5071
Restrooms: Yes   Picnic area: Yes   Public telephone: No
Walks: There are many parkways and a long roadside berm.

Park Walking in San Diego County

Chula Vista   Friendship Park

Description: Beautifully shaded eight acres with exercise trail.
Located at Fourth and "F" Streets, Chula Vista
Transit service: CVT #701, #702/702A, #706/706A
Schedules: 233-3004
Thomas Guide: Page 69, Grid D/3   Street parking
Open: 0700 to 2230   Jurisdiction: City of Chula Vista   691-5071
Restrooms: No   Picnics: Yes   Telephone: No
Walks: There is an interesting exercise trail in this park.

Chula Vista   Greg Rogers Park

Description: 52 Acres of play fields with a community recreation
building, ballfields, totlot and playground.
Located at 1101 Oleander Avenue, Chula Vista
Transit service: CVT #703   Schedules: 233-3004
Thomas Guide: Page 70, Grid B/6   On-site parking
Open: 0600 to 2230   Jurisdiction: City of Chula Vista   691-5071
Restrooms: Yes   Picnic tables: Yes   Public telephone: No
Walks: There are many fine parkways in this facility.

Chula Vista   Hilltop Park

Description: A lovely rolling meadow with numerous shade trees
and a playground on the eleven-acre park site.
Located at 780 Hilltop Drive, Chula Vista
Transit service:CVT #702/702A, #703   Schedules: 233-3004
Thomas Guide: Page 69, Grid F/5   On-site parking
Open: 0700 to 2230   Jurisdiction: City of Chula Vista   691-5071
Restrooms: Yes   Picnic tables: Yes   Public telephone: No
Walks: Excellent paved loop parkways allow intensive walking.

Chula Vista   Horseshoe Park

Description: Mini-park with horseshoe pits and huge old trees.
Located at Del Mar Avenue and Center Street, Chula Vista
Transit service: CVT #702/702A, #706/706A   Info: 233-3004
Thomas Guide: Page 69, Grid D/4   Metered street parking
Open: 0700 to 2230   Jurisdiction: City of Chula Vista   691-5071
Restrooms: No   Picnic table: Yes   Public telephone: No
Walks: The adjoining residential area is recommended.

Chula Vista

Independence Park

Description: Neighborhood park, gentle slopes and play area.
Located at 1248 Calle Santiago, Chula Vista
Transit service: CVT #704   Schedules: 233-3004
Thomas Guide: Page 70, Grid D/4   On-site parking
Open: 0700 to 2230   Jurisdiction: City of Chula Vista   691-5071
Restrooms: No   Picnic area: No   Public telephone: No
Walks: Rolling meadows and nearby areas are fine for walking.

Chula Vista

Los Ninos Park

Description: Neighborhood park with a playground, picnic area.
Located at 150 Teal Street, Chula Vista
Transit service: CVT #701   Schedules: 233-3004
Thomas Guide: Page; 72, Grid B/2   Street parking
Open: 0700 to 2230   Jurisdiction: City of Chula Vista   691-5071
Restrooms: Yes   Picnic area: Yes   Public telephone: No
Walks: In the park site and adjoining residential area.

Chula Vista

Memorial Park

Description: Center-city park with amphitheater, bridges, totlot,
pool, gymnasium, playground, shuffleboard, recreation center.
Located at 385 Parkway, Chula Vista
Transit service: CVT #701, #702, #706/706A   Info: 233-3004
Thomas Guide: Page 69, Grid D/4   Street parking
Open: 0700 to 2230   Jurisdiction: City of Chula Vista   691-5071
Restrooms: Yes   Picnic area: Yes   Public telephone: No
Walks: Pleasant parkways, nearby business/residential areas.

Chula Vista   Norman Park

Description: Small neighborhood park, rec center, shuffleboard.
Located at 270 "F" Street, Chula Vista   Transit Info. 233-3004
Transit service: SDT #29, CVT #701, #702, #706/706A
Thomas Guide: Page 69, Grid D/3   Street parking
Open: 0700 to 2230   Jurisdiction: City of Chula Vista   691-5071
Restrooms: No   Picnic area: Yes   Public telephone: No
Walks: Adjoining area recommended.

Chula Vista   Rancho del Rey Park

Description: Neighborhood play area, tennis, gazebos, totlot.
Located at 1311 Buena Vista Way, Chula Vista
Transit service: CVT #704   Schedules: 233-3004
Thomas Guide: Page 70, Grid E/4   Street parking
Open: 0700 to 2230   Jurisdiction: City of Chula Vista   691-5071
Restrooms: No   Picnic tables/BBQs   Public telephone: No
Walks: Unique serpentine parkway and the nearby residential
area are excellent walking opportunities.

Chula Vista   Rienstra Ball Fields

Description: Six acres of baseball fields.
Located at 1500 Max Avenue, Chula Vista
Transit service: CVT #701   Schedules: 233-3004
Thomas Guide: Page 72, Grid A/1   On-site parking
Open: 0700 to 2230   Jurisdiction: City of Chula Vista   691-5071
Restrooms: Yes   Picnic area: No   Public telephone: No
Walks: Nearby area is best unless ball fields are not in use.

Park Walking in San Diego County

City Heights   **Azalea Park**

Description: Neighborhood recreation center and totlot.
Located at 2596 Violet Street, San Diego
Transit service: No
Thomas Guide: Page 61, Grid B/5   On-site parking
Open: 24 Hours   Jurisdiction: City of San Diego   283-7880
Restrooms: Yes   Picnic tables: Yes   Public telephone: Yes
Walks: Paved parkways and the nearby area are walkable.

City Heights   **City Heights Community Park**

Description: Recreation center, play fields, ball courts and totlot.
Located at 4777 44th Street, San Diego
Transit service: No
Thomas Guide: Page 61, Grid B/2   On-site parking
Open: 24 Hours   Jurisdiction: City of San Diego   283-2574
Restrooms: Yes   Picnic tables/BBQs   Public telephone: No
Walks: Park not suitable but the nearby area is.

City Heights   **City Heights Mini-Park**

Description: Playground equipment and large gazebo.
Located at 3033 39th Street, San Diego
Transit service: SDT #7, #13   Schedules: 233-3004
Thomas Guide: Page 61, Grid B/5   Street parking
Open: 24 Hours   Jurisdiction: City of San Diego   236-6661
Restrooms: No   Picnic table: Yes   Public telephone: No
Walks: Not recommended. No parkways and streets are narrow.

City Heights   **Hollywood Park**

Description: Isolated park of fields and playground equipment.
Located at 2301 Shamrock Street, San Diego
Transit service: SDT #13   Schedules: 233-3004
Thomas Guide: Page 61, Grid B/5   Limited street parking
Open: 24 Hours   Jurisdiction: City of San Diego   236-6661
Restrooms: Yes   Picnic tables: Yes   Public telephone: No
Walks: Park and adjoining area are not suitable for walking.

Clairemont   Cadman Park

Description: Recreation center, neighborhood park and totlot.
Located at 4280 Avanti Drive, San Diego
Transit service: No
Thomas Guide: Page 52, Grid D/2   On-site parking
Open: 24 Hours   Jurisdiction: City of San Diego   490-0921
Restrooms: Yes   Picnic tables/BBQs   Public telephone: No
Walks: Limited potential in park but residential area is useful.

Clairemont   East Clairemont Athletic Area

Description: A complex of ballfields and associated outbuildings.
Located at 3451 Mount Acadia Boulevard, San Diego
Transit service: No
Thomas Guide: Page 53, Grid A/3   On-site parking
Open: 24 Hours   Jurisdiction: City of San Diego   236-6661
Restrooms: No   Picnic area: No   Public telephone: No
Walks: Barren fields and adjacent streets not suitable.

Clairemont   Gershwin Park

Description: Nice neighborhood park, tennis, totlot, shade trees.
Located at 3505 Conrad Avenue, San Diego
Transit service: SDT #4, #25, #50/150   Schedules: 233-3004
Thomas Guide: Page 44, Grid E/6   Street parking
Open: 24 Hours   Jurisdiction: City of San Diego   236-6661
Restrooms: No   Picnic tables: Yes   Public telephone: No
Walks: The nearby residential area is recommended.

Clairemont   Lindbergh Park

Description: Community site, tennis, playground, shade trees.
Located at 4141 Ashford Street, San Diego
Transit service: SDT #4, #27   Schedules: 233-3004
Thomas Guide: Page 53, Grid C/2   Street parking
Open: 24 Hours   Jurisdiction: City of San Diego   236-6661
Restrooms: Yes   Picnic tables/BBQs   Public telephone: No
Walks: Excellent park turf, paved parkways and adjoining area.

Clairemont   Mac Dowell Park

Description: Small neighborhood park with nice playground.
Located at 5183 Arvinels Avenue, San Diego
Transit service: No
Thomas Guide: Page 45, Grid B/5   Street parking
Open: 24 Hours   Jurisdiction: City of San Diego   236-6661
Restrooms: No   Picnic tables: Yes   Public telephone: No
Walks: On the paved parkway, in the nearby residential area.

Clairemont   Marion Bear Memorial Park

Description: This is a large urban natural park with a fine
network of lengthy trails. Also known as San Clemente Canyon.
Located on Clairemont Mesa Blvd. So. of Highway 52, San Diego
Transit service: SDT #41   Schedules: 233-3004
Thomas Guide: Page 44, Grid D/5   Multiple on-site parking lots
Open: 24 Hours   Jurisdiction: City of San Diego   236-6661
Restrooms: Yes   Picnic tables/BBQs   Public telephone: No
Walking: This is a major complex of well-used walking trails.

Clairemont   Mount Acadia Park

Description: Gently sloping parksite, playground and totlot.
Located at 3865 Mount Acadia Boulevard, San Diego
Transit service: SDT #27, #41   Schedules: 233-3304
Thomas Guide: Page 53, Grid B/2   Street parking
Open: 24 Hours   Jurisdiction: City of San Diego   236-3004
Restrooms: Yes   Picnic tables/BBQs   Public telephone: No
Walks: Suitable for parkland and residential area walking.

Clairemont   Mount Etna Park

Description: Multi-level park with playing fields and totlot.
Located at 4741 Mount Etna Drive, San Diego
Transit service: SDT #41   Schedules: 233-3004
Thomas Guide: Page 53, Grid A/1   On-site parking
Open: 24 Hours   Jurisdiction: City of San Diego   236-6661
Restrooms: Yes   Picnic area: Yes   Public telephone: No
Walks: For exercise walking use parkways and area sidewalks.

Clairemont

North Clairemont Park

Description: Neighborhood play fields, ball courts, tennis, totlot.
Located at 4421 Bannock Avenue, San Diego
Transit service: SDT #4, #25, #41, #50/150   Schedules: 233-3004
Thomas Guide: Page 44, Grid F/6   Street parking
Open: 24 Hours   Jurisdiction: City of San Diego   490-0926
Restrooms: No   Picnic tables: Yes   Public telephone: No
Walks: Nice parkways and entrance to nearby Tecolate Canyon.

Clairemont

Olive Grove Community Park

Description: Tennis, playground, totlot, many fine shade trees.
Located at 6075 Printwood Way, San Diego
Transit service: SDT #4   Schedules: 233-3004
Thomas Guide: Page 53, Grid B/1   Limited on-site parking
Open: 24 Hours   Jurisdiction: City of San Diego   236-6661
Restrooms: Yes   Picnic tables: Yes   Public telephone: No
Walks: Grassed parkland and paved parkways are excellent.

Clairemont

South Clairemont Park

Description: Rec. center, pool, ball court, playground and totlot.
Located at 3605 Clairemont Drive, San Diego
Transit service: SDT #5/105, #27, #50/150   Schedules: 233-3004
Thomas Guide: Page 52, Grid F/3   Street parking
Open: 24 Hours   Jurisdiction: City of San Diego   490-0924
Restrooms: Yes   Picnic tables/BBQs   Public telephone: No
Walks: Try paved parkways and residential area for walking.

Coronado

Centennial Park

Description: Bayfront mini-park with fine San Diego City view.
Located at 1100 First Street, Coronado
Transit service: MTS #901   Schedules: 233-3004
Thomas Guide: Page 65, Grid B/3   Metered street parking
Open: 24 Hours   Jurisdiction: City of Coronado   522-7342
Restrooms: No   Picnic area: No   Public telephone: No
Walks: Behind park is an excellent bayfront paved parkway.

Coronado   Glorietta Bay Park

Description: Neighborhood bayfront park, totlot, excellent view.
Located at 1975 Strand Way, Coronado
Transit service: MTS #901   Schedules: 233-3004
Thomas Guide: Page 65, Grid C/6   On-site parking.
Open: 24 Hours   Jurisdiction: City of Coronado   522-7342
Restrooms: No   Picnic tables: Yes   Public telephone: No
Walks: There are long bayfront paved paths and a bike route.

Coronado   South Bay County Marine Study Area

Description: Interesting area for study of tidewater marshlands.
Located on Silver Strand Boulevard, Coronado. (Sign posted)
Transit service: MTS #901   Schedules: 233-3004
Thomas Guide: Page 70-Z, Grid F/2   On-site parking
Open: 24 Hours   Jurisdiction: County of San Diego   694-3049
Restrooms: No   Picnic area: No   Public telephone: No
Walks: Adjoins an excellent paved bikeway along the bay front.

Coronado   Spreckels Park

Description: Grassed city block, playground, totlot, shade trees.
Located at Seventh and "C" Streets, Coronado
Transit service: MTS #901   Schedules: 233-3004
Thomas Guide: Page 65, Grid B/4   Street parking
Open: 24 Hours   Jurisdiction: City of Coronado   522-7342
Restrooms: Yes   Picnic tables: Yes   Public telephone: No
Walks: Use of the nearby residential area is recommended.

Coronado   Star Park

Description: This is the landscaped center of a traffic circle.
At joining of Star Park Place, Loma Ave, Park Place; Coronado
Transit service: MTS #901   Schedules: 233-3004
Thomas Guide: Page 65, Grid B/5   Limited street parking
Open: 24 Hours   Jurisdiction: City of Coronado   522-7342
Restrooms: No   Picnic area: No   Public telephone: No
Walks: Use of the residential area is all that is possible.

Coronado   **Sunset Park**

Description: Small neighborhood park at entry to North Island.
Located at Ocean Boulevard and Ocean Drive, Coronado
Transit service: No
Thomas Guide: Page 65, Grid A/4   Street parking
Open: 24 Hours   Jurisdiction: City of Coronado   694-3049
Restrooms: No   Picnic area: No   Public telephone: No
Walks: Limited in the park. Nearby beach-front walk is better.

Coronado   **Tidelands Park**

Description: A beautiful park adjacent to the Bay Bridge with a
spectacular harbor view, tennis, ball court, playground, totlot.
Located on Mullinix Drive, Coronado
Transit service: MTS #901   Schedules: 233-3004
Thomas Guide: Page 65, Grid C/4   Plentiful on-site parking
Open: 24 Hours   Jurisdiction: Port of San Diego   291-3900
Restrooms: Yes   Picnic tables: Yes   Public telephone: No
Walks: A few short parkways, excellent paved bayfront paths.

Corridor   **Park de La Cruz**

Description: Poorly maintained canyon park with ball courts.
Located at 3901 Landis Street, San Diego
Transit service: SDT #7   Schedules: 233-3004
Thomas Guide: Page 61, Grid B/4   Limited street parking
Open: 24 Hours   Jurisdiction: City of San Diego   236-6661
Restrooms: No   Picnic area: No   Public telephone: No
Walks: Not recommended. Congested area and rough parkways.

Corridor   **Wabash Park**

Description: Triangle mini-park amid busy boulevards.
Located at University Avenue and Wabash Street, San Diego
Transit service: SDT #6, #7   Schedules: 233-3004
Thomas Guide: Page 61, Grid A/3   Limited street parking
Open: 24 Hours   Jurisdiction: City of San Diego   236-6661
Restrooms: No   Picnic table: Yes   Public telephone: No
Walks: Not recommended due to size and surrounding traffic.

Cottonwood   **Cottonwood 1 County Park**

Description: Grassed five-acre parksite with shaded perimeter.
Located at Windriver Road and Brabham Street, El Cajon
Transit service: No
Thomas Guide: Page 63-P, Grid A/3   Street parking
Open: 24 Hours   Jurisdiction: County of San Diego   694-3049
Restrooms: No   Picnic area: No   Public telephone: No
Walks: On grassed parkland, the parkway or residential area.

Cottonwood   **Cottonwood 2 County Park**

Description: Eight acres of undeveloped parkland.
Located at 1995 Donahue Drive, El Cajon
Transit service: No
Thomas Guide: Page 63-P, Grid A/3   Street parking
Open: Not open   Jurisdiction: County of San Diego   694-3049
Restrooms: No   Picnic area: No   Public telephone: No
Walks: Undeveloped park site not suitable for walking ventures.

Cottonwood   **Cottonwood 3 County Park**

Description: This is a ten-acre undeveloped park site.
Located at Hilton Head Road and Muirfield Drive, El Cajon
Transit service: No
Thomas Guide: Page 63, Grid F/4   Street parking
Open: Not open   Jurisdiction: County of San Diego   694-3049
Restrooms: No   Picnic area: No   Public telephone: No
Walks: Undeveloped park site not suitable for walking ventures.

Crest   Nancy Jane County Park

Description: Seldom used little park; tennis, totlot, ball court.
Located at 1400 La Cresta Boulevard, El Cajon
Transit service: CTS #888   Schedules: 233-3004
Thomas Guide: Page 57, Grid E/2   Street parking
Open: 24 Hours   Jurisdiction: County of San Diego   694-3049
Restrooms: Yes   Picnic tables/BBQs   Public telephone: No
Walks: Two-acre park site not recommended. No area sidewalks.

Crest   South Lane Park

Description: Large natural site with horse ring.
Located at 100 Albatross Place, El Cajon
Transit service: No
Thomas Guide: Page 57, Grid E/3   On-site parking
Open: 24 Hours   Jurisdiction: County of San Diego   694-3049
Restrooms: No   Picnic area: No   Public telephone: No
Walks: Site not suitable. There are no area sidewalks.

Cuyamaca   Cuyamaca Rancho State Park

Description: Camping, nature center and fishing, 26,000 acres.
Located at 12551 Highway 79, Cuyamaca
Transit service: CTS #885   Schedules: 233-3004
Thomas Guide: Page 28-W, Grid C/3   On-site parking
Open: Dawn to dusk   Jurisdiction: State of California   765-0755
Restrooms: Yes   Picnic tables/BBQs   Telephone: Yes
Walks: Over 100 miles of maintained trails for outdoor exercise.

Del Cerro   Navajo Open Space Preserve

Description: Undeveloped open space. Not for public use.
Located at intersection of Navajo Road and College Avenue, SD
Transit service: SDT #13, #115   Schedules: 233-3004
Thomas Guide: Page 54, Grid E/4   Street parking
Open: Closed to public use   Jurisdiction: City of San Diego
Information: 256-6731   Restrooms: No   Benches: No
Picnic area: No   Public Telephone: No   Walks: No

Del Cerro   **Princess Del Cerro Neighborhood Park**

Description: Small grassed park, playing fields and tot lot.
Located at 6195 Wenrich Drive, San Diego
Transit service: SDT #13, # 115   Schedules: 233-3004
Thomas Guide: Page 54, Grid E/5   Street parking
Open: 24-Hours   Jurisdiction: City of San Diego   236-6661
Restrooms: No   Picnic tables: Yes   Public telephone: No
Walks: Residential area walking would be best.

Del Dios   **Lake Hodges**

Description: A large lake, boat launching facilities, on 1575
acres of recreational parkland. Fishing allowed with day permit.
Located off Lake Drive in the Del Dios area of San Diego
Transit service: NCTD # 384   Schedules: 722 or 743-6283
Thomas Guide: Page 27, Grid B/1   Adequate on-site parking
Open: Dawn to dusk, Wednesday, Saturday and Sunday only
Jurisdiction: City of San Diego   465-3474   Restrooms: Yes
Picnic tables: Yes   Telephone: Yes   Walks: Many fine trails.

Eastlake   **Bonita-Long Canyon Park**

Description: A natural canyon site with random hiking trails.
Located on Corral Canyon Road, at Port Renwick, Chula Vista
Transit service: CVT #705A   Schedules: 233-3004
Thomas Guide: Page 70, Grid F/2   Street parking
Open: 24 Hours   Jurisdiction: City of Chula Vista   691-5071
Restrooms: No   Picnic area: No   Public telephone: No
Walks: Look for a Trail marker on west side of Corral Canyon.

Eastlake   **Tiffany Park**

Description: Very nice seven-acre hillslope, playground, totlot.
Located at 1731 Elmhurst Street, Chula Vista
Transit service: CVT #705, #705A   Schedules: 233-3004
Thomas Guide: Page 70, Grid F/3   Street parking
Open: 0700 to 2230   Jurisdiction: City of Chula Vista   691-5071
Restrooms: No   Picnic tables: Yes   Public telephone: No
Walks: Fine paved parkways and nearby residential areas.

Eden Gardens   **La Colonia Park**

Description: Small neighborhood play field with bleachers.
Located at 600 Stevens Avenue, Solana Beach
Transit service: NCTD #308   Schedules: 722 or 743-6283
Thomas Guide: Page 30, Grid A/5   Street parking
Open: 0800 to 2100 Jurisdiction: City of Solana Beach 755-2998
Restrooms: No   Picnic tables: Yes   Public telephone: No
Walks: There are short parkways and heavy area traffic.

El Cajon   **Bill Beck Park**

Description: Mini-park, playground, ball court and totlot.
Located at Pierce Street and Wagner Drive, El Cajon
Transit service: SDT # 115   Schedules: 233-3004
Also: CTS #846, #847, #848, #852, #858, #864
Thomas Guide: Page 56, Grid A/3   Street parking
Open: 0700 to 2200   Jurisdiction: City of El Cajon   441-1754
Restrooms: No   Picnic table: Yes   Public telephone: No
Walks: Area residential sidewalks only. Mini-park is too small.

El Cajon   **John F. Kennedy Park**

Description: Rec. center, gym, tennis, ball courts, shade trees.
Located at 1675 East Madison Avenue, El Cajon
Transit service: SDT #15   Schedules: 233-3004
Thomas Guide: Page 56, Grid F/4   On-site parking
Open: 0700 to 2200   Jurisdiction: City of El Cajon   441-1676
Restrooms: Yes   Picnic tables: Yes   Public telephone: Yes
Walks: Many fine paved parkways and nearby residential area.

El Cajon   **Judson Park**

Description: Tiny center-city corner lot with shaded gazebo.
Located at 300 Magnolia Avenue, El Cajon
Transit service: SDT #15, #115, CTS # 864   Schedules: 233-3004
Thomas Guide: Page 56, Grid B/4   Limited street parking
Open: 24 Hours   Jurisdiction: City of El Cajon   441-1754
Restrooms: No   Picnic tables: Yes   Public telephone: No
Walks: Not suitable for walks in the heavily congested area.

El Cajon   Junior High School Park

Description: Playing fields and parkland shared with school use.
Located at 400 Park Avenue, El Cajon
Transit service: CTS #852   Schedules: 233-3004
Thomas Guide: Page 56, Grid C/4   On-site parking
Open: 0700 to 2200   Jurisdiction: City of El Cajon   441-1754
Restrooms: Yes   Picnic area: No   Public telephone: Yes
Walks: Use the paved parkway and adjoining residential area.

El Cajon   Renette Park

Description: Rec center, gymnasium, turf, playground and totlot.
Located at 935 South Emerald Avenue, El Cajon
Transit service: CTS #852   Schedules: 233-3004
Thomas Guide: Page 56, Grid B/5   On-site parking
Open: 0700 to 2200   Jurisdiction: City of El Cajon   441-1678
Restrooms: Yes   Picnic tables/BBQs   Public telephone: Yes
Walks: Short parkway and grassed parksite fields only.

El Cajon   Wells Park

Description: Recreation center, PAR course, horseshoes, play
area and totlot in a very nice parksite.
Located at 1153 East Madison Avenue, El Cajon
Transit service: SDT #15   Schedules: 233-3004
Thomas Guide: Page 56, Grid D/4   On-site parking
Open: 0700 to 2230   Jurisdiction: City of El Cajon   441-1680
Restrooms: Yes   Picnic tables/BBQs   Public telephone: No
Walks: Paved parkways, grass fields and the adjoining area.

El Capitan

El Capitan Reservoir

Description: Water storage lake offering fishing and hiking.
Located at the end of El Monte Road, Lakeside
Transit service: No
Thomas Guide: Page 405, Grid B/5   On-site parking
Open: Friday-Sunday   Jurisdiction: City of San Diego   465-3474
Restrooms: Yes   Picnic area: Yes   Public telephone: Yes
Walks: There are many natural trails in the area.

El Centro (Imperial)

Adams Avenue Park

Description: Long grassed park strip, playground, tennis, totlot.
Located at 700 Adams Avenue, El Centro
Transit service: Yes   Schedules: Goodall's 353-3520
Thomas Guide: Page 410, Grid D/3   Street parking
Open: 24 Hours   Jurisdiction: City of El Centro   337-4557
Restrooms: Yes   Picnic tables/BBQs   Public telephone: No
Walks: Heavy area traffic and no parkways limit exercise walks.

El Centro (Imperial)

Bucklin Park

Description: Large shaded park, pond, playground and totlot.
Located at Ross Avenue and Eighth Street, El Centro
Transit service: Yes   Schedules: Goodall's 353-3520
Thomas Guide: Page 410, Grid D/4   On-site parking
Open: 24 Hours   Jurisdiction: City of El Centro   337-4557
Restrooms: Yes   Picnic tables/BBQs   Public telephone: No
Walks: There is a fine loop parkway and numerous paths in this
facility, as well as a pleasant adjacent residential area.

El Centro (Imperial)   **Carlos Aguilar Park**

Description: Neighborhood park, grass ballfields, gazebo, totlot.
Located at 125 Pico Avenue, El Centro
Transit service: Yes   Schedules: Goodall's 353-3520
Thomas Guide: Page 410, Grid C/2   On-site parking
Open: 24 Hours   Jurisdiction: City of El Centro   337-4557
Restrooms: Yes   Picnic tables/BBQs   Public telephone: No
Walks: Best in the park when ball fields are not in use.

El Centro (Imperial)   **Debbi Pittmark Park**

Description: Baseball fields with very little grass or shade.
Located at 1947 Orange Avenue, El Centro
Transit service: Yes   Schedules: Goodall's 353-3520
Thomas Guide: Page 410, Grid C/4   Street parking
Open: 24 Hours   Jurisdiction: City of El Centro   337-4557
Restrooms: No   Picnic area: No   Public telephone: No
Walks: Not recommended due to park use, heavy area traffic.

El Centro (Imperial)   **Eddie White Complex**

Description: Multiple earth ballfields without shade trees.
Located at Sandy Avenue and Sixth Street, El Centro
Transit service: Yes   Schedules: Goodall's 353-3520
Thomas Guide: Page 410, Grid D/2   On-site parking
Open: 24 Hours   Jurisdiction: City of El Centro   337-4557
Restrooms: Yes   Picnic area: No   Public telephone: No
Walks: Only in park site when baseball fields are not in use.

El Centro (Imperial)   **McGee Park**

Description: Recreation center, ball fields, playground, totlot.
Located at 375 South First Street, El Centro
Transit service: Yes   Schedules: Goodall's 353-3520
Thomas Guide: Page 410, Grid E/3   Street parking
Open: 24 Hours   Jurisdiction: City of El Centro   337-4557
Restrooms: Yes   Picnic tables/BBQs   Public telephone: No
Walks: Residential area walking is recommended.

El Centro (Imperial)   **Stark Field**

Description: Huge baseball complex, shaded playground, totlot.
Located at Fourth Street and Hamilton Avenue, El Centro
Transit service: Yes   Schedules: Goodall's 353-3520
Thomas Guide: Page 410, Grid E/4   On-site parking
Open: 24 Hours   Jurisdiction: City of El Centro   337-4557
Restrooms: Yes   Picnic tables/BBQs   Public telephone: No
Walks: Not suitable for walking when ball fields are in use.

El Centro (Imperial)   **Swarthout Park**

Description: Lightly grassed ballfields, playground and totlot.
Located at Euclid Avenue and Fourth Street, El Centro
Transit service: Yes   Schedules: Goodall's 353-3520
Thomas Guide: Page 410, Grid E/2   On-site parking
Open: 24 Hours   Jurisdiction: City of El Centro   337-4557
Restrooms: Yes   Picnic tables/BBQs   Public telephone: No
Walks: Not suitable for walking when ball fields are in use.

Encanto   **Emerald Hills Park**

Description: Grassed expanse, ball court, tennis and totlot.
Located on Bethune Court off Kelton Road, San Diego
Transit service: No
Thomas Guide: Page 61, Grid E/6   Street parking
Open: 24 Hours   Jurisdiction: City of San Diego   236-6661
Restrooms: Yes   Picnic tables: Yes   Public telephone: No
Walks: Enjoy the excellent parkways and residential areas.

Encanto   **Encanto Community Park**

Description: Senior Center, tennis, ball courts and totlot.
Located at 6508 Wunderlin Avenue, San Diego
Transit service: SDT #16   Schedules: 233-3004
Thomas Guide: Page 66, Grid F/1   Street parking
Open: 24 Hours   Jurisdiction: City of San Diego   262-5489
Restrooms: Yes   Picnic tables: Yes   Public telephone: No
Walks: Paved parkways and the nearby area are recommended.

Encanto

Encanto Park

Description: Modest park with mature shade trees, playground.
Located at 6715 Imperial Avenue, San Diego
Transit service: SDT #4   Schedules: 233-3004
Thomas Guide: Page 67, Grid A/2   On-site parking
Open: 24 Hours   Jurisdiction: City of San Diego   236-6661
Restrooms: No   Picnic tables: Yes   Public telephone: No
Walks: There are gentle grassed slopes, a minimum of parkway.

Encinitas

Cardiff-By-The-Sea Sports Park

Description: Baseball, soccer, playfield and playground.
Located at 1661 Lake Drive, Encinitas
Transit service: NCTD #361   Schedules: 722 or 743-6283
Thomas Guide: Page 30, Grid A/1   On-site parking
Open: Dawn to dusk Jurisdiction: Encinitas and Cardiff Schools
Information: 944-3380   Restrooms: Yes   Picnic tables: Yes
Telephone: Yes   Walks: Excellent, when ball fields not in use.

Encinitas

Encinitas Viewpoint Park

Description: Delightful park with ocean view, playground, totlot.
Located at 60 East "D" Street, Encinitas
Transit service: NCTD #301, #361   Schedules: 722 or 743-6283
Thomas Guide: Page 24, Grid E/4   Limited street parking
Open: Dawn to dusk   Jurisdiction: City of Encinitas   944-3380
Restrooms: No   Picnic tables: Yes   Public telephone: No
Walks: Steep park slopes make the nearby area more suitable.

Encinitas   Glen Park

Description: Community park, baseball, playing field and totlot.
Located at 2149 Orinda Drive, Encinitas
Transit service: NCTD #302, #304, #308, #309, #310, #361
Schedules: 722 or 743-6283
Thomas Guide: Page 29, Grid B/2   On-site parking
Open: Dawn to dusk   Jurisdiction: City of Encinitas   944-5050
Restrooms: Yes   Picnic tables/BBQs   Public telephone: Yes
Walks: There are parkways, the area and nearby ocean beach.

Encinitas   Oakcrest Park

Description: Hilltop with ocean breeze, totlot and play fields.
Located at 1140 Oakcrest Park Drive, Encinitas
Transit service: NCTD #309, #361   Schedules: 722 or 743-6283
Thomas Guide: Page 25, Grid A/5   On-site parking
Open: Dawn to dusk   Jurisdiction: City of Encinitas 944-3380
Restrooms: Yes   Picnic tables/BBQs   Public telephone: No
Walks: Excellent loop parkway and nearby residential area.

Encinitas   Quail Botanical Gardens

Description: Thirty acres of carefully identified exotic plants.
Located at 230 Quail Gardens Drive, Encinitas
Transit service: NCTD #361   Schedules: 722 or 743-6283
Thomas Guide: Page 24, Grid E/3-4   On-site parking fee
Open: 0800 to 1700 Jurisdiction: County of San Diego 694-3049
Restrooms: Yes   Picnic area: No   Public telephone: Yes
Walks: Many parkways for strolling. Area walks not feasible.

Encinitas   San Elijo Lagoon County Park

Description: Almost 1000 acres for nature study, birdwatching.
Located at 1000 Santa Helena Drive, Lomas Santa Fe
Transit service: No   (Note: Address is on Page 30, Grid B/4)
Thomas Guide: Page 30, Grid B/3 (Park location) Street parking
Open: 0930 to 1700 Jurisdiction: County of San Diego 694-3049
Restrooms: No   Picnic area: No   Public telephone: No
Walks: Nature trails, more pleasant for hiking than walking.

Escondido   Dixon Lake Recreation Area

Description: A 70-acre lake in a lovely 520-acre regional park.
Camping, playground, horseshoes, ball court, horse arena, totlot.
Located at 1700 La Honda Drive, Escondido
Transit service: No
Thomas Guide: Page 18, Grid B/4   Plentiful on-site parking
Open: Dawn to dusk   Jurisdiction: City of Escondido   741-4680
Restrooms: Yes   Picnic tables/BBQs   Public telephone: Yes
Walking: A variety of maintained and natural walking trails.

Escondido   Felicita County Park

Description: 52-Acres, ballfields, tot-lots, playgrounds, shade.
Located at 742 Clarence Lane, Escondido
Transit service: No
Thomas Guide: Page 27, Grid D/1   On-site parking fee
Open: 0930 to 1700 Jurisdiction: County of San Diego 694-3049
Restrooms: Yes   Picnic tables/BBQs   Public telephone: Yes
Walking: There are a number of fine walking and hiking trails.

Escondido   Grape Day Park

Description: Center-city community park, 21 acres, historic
buildings, ballfield, recreation building, pool and PAR course.
Located at 321 North Broadway, Escondido
Transit service: NCTD #381, #382, #384   Info. 722 or 743-6283
Thomas Guide: Page 22, Grid D/2   Street parking
Open: Dawn to 2200   Jurisdiction: City of Escondido 741-4691
Restrooms: Yes   Picnic tables/BBQs   Public telephone: Yes.
Walking: Long open paved parkways or business area sidewalks.

Escondido   **Kit Carson Park**

Description: A 285-acre park with amphitheater, tennis, pool, rec center, playing fields, totlot, baseball and playground.
Located at 3333 Bear Valley Parkway, Escondido
Transit service: NCTD #384   Schedules: 722 or 743-6283
Thomas Guide: Page 27, Grid F/2   Plentiful on-site parking
Open: Dawn to 2200   Jurisdiction: City of Escondido   741-4691
Restrooms: Yes   Picnic tables/BBQs   Public telephone: Yes
Walking: There are maintained nature trails and park paths.

Escondido   **Mountain View Park**

Description: Tennis, play fields, baseball, soccer and totlot.
Located at 1160 South Citrus Avenue, Escondido
Transit service: NCTD # 381   Schedules: 722 or 743-6283
Thomas Guide: Page 23, Grid B/2   On site parking
Open: Dawn to 2200 Jurisdiction: City of Escondido 741-4691
Restrooms: Yes   Picnic tables: Yes   Public telephone: Yes
Walking: Nearby area sidewalks are best walking opportunities.

Escondido   **Open Space County Park**

Description: Undeveloped open space. Closed to public use.
Located on Morning View Drive between Lincoln and El Norte
Transit service: No
Thomas Guide: Page 22, Grid D/1
Open: Closed   Jurisdiction: City of Escondido   741-4691
Restrooms: No   Picnic area: No   Public Telephone: No
Walks: Not suitable for walking ventures.

Escondido   **Rock Springs Neighborhood Park**

Description: Undeveloped open space. Closed to public use
Located at intersection of Rock Springs Road and Seven Oaks
Transit service: No
Thomas Guide: Page 22, Grid C/1
Open: Closed   Jurisdiction: City of Escondido   741-4691
Restrooms: No   Picnic area: No   Public Telephone: No
Walks: Not suitable for walking ventures.

Escondido

Rod McCleod Park

Description: Delightful hilltop site, playground and totlot.
Located at 1791 South Iris Lane, Escondido
Transit service: NCTD #385   Schedules: 722 or 743-6283
Thomas Guide: Page 17 Grid C/5   On-site parking
Open: Dawn to 2200   Jurisdiction: City of Escondido   741-4691
Restrooms: Yes   Picnic tables/BBQs   Public telephone: No
Walks: The paved parkway loop is best. Area walks not feasible.

Escondido

Washington Park

Description: Baseball, tennis, ball court, rec building and totlot.
Located at 501 North Rose, Escondido
Transit service: NCTD #381, #385   Schedules: 722 or 743-6283
Thomas Guide: Page 22, Grid F/1   Limited on-site parking
Open: Dawn to 2200. Jurisdiction: City of Escondido   741-4691
Restrooms: Yes   Picnic tables/BBQs Public Telephone: Yes.
Walks: Area sidewalks offer the best walking opportunities.

Escondido

Westside Park

Description: Small neighborhood park, playground and totlot.
Located at 333 Spruce Street, Escondido
Transit service: NCTD #382   Schedules: 722 or 743-6283
Thomas Guide: Page 22, Grid D/3   Street parking
Open: Dawn to 2200   Jurisdiction: City of Escondido   741-4691
Restrooms: Yes   Picnic tables/BBQs   Public telephone: No
Walks: Not recommended. Few area sidewalks and no parkways.

Fallbrook

Fallbrook Community Park

Description: Community center with tennis courts, playground, ball courts, and totlot on a six-acre neighborhood site.
Located at 341 Heald Lane, Fallbrook.
Transit service: NCTD Fallbrook FAST   Schedules: 728-4333
Thomas Guide: Page 1-5, Grid D/4   Street parking
Open: 0900-2200   Jurisdiction: County of San Diego 723-8838
Restrooms: Yes   Picnic area: No   Public telephone: Yes
Walking: Surrounding area sidewalks offer the best option.

Fallbrook

Live Oak County Park

Description: A lovely wooded valley of 25 acres with play fields, totlot, playground, horseshoes and ball court.
Located at 2700 Reche Road by Gird Road, Fallbrook.
Transit service: NCTD Fallbrook FAST.   Schedules: 728-4333
Thomas Guide: Page 1-5 Grid F/5   On-site parking fee
Open: 0930-1830. Jurisdiction: County of San Diego 694-3049
Restrooms: Yes   Picnic tables/BBQs   Public telephone: No
Walking: There are numerous well-used walking paths.

Fletcher Hills

Fletcher Hills Mini-Park & Pool

Description: Tiny lunch-table park behind the city pool building.
Located at 2345 Center Place, El Cajon
Transit service: SDT #115   Schedules: 233-3004
Thomas Guide: Page 55, Grid F/3   Street parking
Open: Call first   Jurisdiction: City of El Cajon   441-1672
Restrooms: Inside Picnic tables: Yes Public Telephone: Inside
Walks: Only the residential area is suitable for walking.

Fletcher Hills

Hillside Park

Description: A beautiful park and community center complex, gymnasium, grassed playfields, totlot and hillside parkways.
Located at 840 Buena Terrace, El Cajon
Transit service: SDT #115 and CTS #858   Schedules: 233-3004
Thomas Guide: Page 55, Grid F/3   On-site parking
Open: 0700 to 2200   Jurisdiction: City of El Cajon   441-1674
Restrooms: Yes   Picnic tables/BBQs   Public telephone: Yes
Walking: A nice selection of paved and well-used parkways.

Flinn Springs

Flinn Springs County Park

Description: Rustic park, ballfields, horseshoes, play and totlot.
Located at 14787 Old Highway 80, El Cajon
Transit service: CTS #864   Schedules: 233-3004
Thomas Guide: Page 49, Grid E/4   On-site parking fee
Open: 0930 to 1700 Jurisdiction: County of San Diego 694-3049
Restrooms: Yes   Picnic tables/BBQs   Public telephone: No
Walks: Many fine parksite trails in the 42-acre wooded valley.

Foster

San Vicente Reservoir Recreation Station

Description: Lake fishing in a water storage facility.
Located at 13500 Moreno Avenue off Vigilante Road, Lakeside
Transit service: No
Thomas Guide: Page 42, Grid E/2   On-site parking
Open: Thur, Sat, Sun only   Jurisdiction: City of S D   465-3474
Restrooms: Yes   Picnic area: No   Telephone: Yes
Walks: Natural trails are in the surrounding terrain.

Foster
Sycamore Canyon County Park

Description: A major undeveloped park site open to hikers.
Located on Highway 67 at Sycamore Park Drive, Lakeside
Transit service: No
Thomas Guide: Page 37-N, Grid B/5   Locked gate
Open: To hikers   Jurisdiction: County of San Diego   694-3049
Restrooms: No   Picnic area: No   Public telephone: No
Walks: Suitable only for experienced hikers.

Golden Hill
Dennis V. Allen Park

Description: Ball court, playground, in pleasant neighborhood.
Located at 800 Boundary Street, San Diego
Transit service: SDT #5/105, #16   Schedules: 233-3004
Thomas Guide: Page 66, Grid A/1   Street parking
Open: 24 Hours   Jurisdiction: City of San Diego   236-6661
Restrooms: Yes   Picnic tables: Yes   Public telephone: No
Walks: On parkways and in the nearby modern industrial area.

Golden Hill
Golden Hill Recreation Center

Description: Rec center, playground, totlot, ball courts and golf.
Located at 2600 Golf Course Drive, San Diego
Transit service: SDT #2   Schedules: 233-3004
Thomas Guide: Page 65, Grid E/1   On-site parking
Open: 24 Hours   Jurisdiction: City of San Diego   239-8533
Restrooms: Yes   Picnic area: No   Public telephone: No
Walks: Walking opportunities are in adjoining Balboa Park.

Golden Hill
"J" Street Mini-Park

Description: Tiny neighborhood park with a totlot.
Located at 3291 "J" Street, San Diego
Transit service: SDT #4, #5/105, #16   Schedules: 233-3004
Thomas Guide: Page 65, Grid F/2   Street parking
Open: 24 Hours   Jurisdiction: City of San Diego   236-6661
Restrooms: No   Picnic tables: Yes   Public telephone: No
Walks: Tiny park and congested traffic area. Not recommended.

Golden Hill

Description: Inner-city corner lot with a ball court.
Located at 2901 "L" Street, San Diego
Transit service: SDT #4   Schedules: 233-3004
Thomas Guide: Page 65, Grid F/2   Street parking
Open: 24 Hours   Jurisdiction: City of San Diego   236-6661
Restrooms: No   Picnic table: Yes   Public telephone: No
Walks: Not suitable; heavy traffic and small one-lot parksite.

Grantville

Grantville Neighborhood Park

Description: A small park with totlot and playing fields.
Located at 4601 Vandever Avenue, San Diego
Transit service: SDT #13, #43   Schedules: 233-3004
Thomas Guide: Page 54. Grid C/5   Street parking
Open: 24-Hours   Jurisdiction: City of San Diego   236-6661
Restrooms: No   Picnic tables: Yes   Public telephone: No
Walks: Area residential walking best as parkways are short.

Grossmont

Briercrest Park

Description: Seven acres, playing fields, totlot and exercise pads.
Located in the 9000 block of Wakarusa Street, La Mesa
Transit service: SDT #15, CTS #854   Schedules: 233-3004
Thomas Guide: Page 55, Grid E/6   Scarce street parking
Open: Dawn to dusk   Jurisdiction: City of La Mesa   469-4128
Restrooms: Yes   Picnic tables: Yes   Public telephone: No
Walks: No parkways and heavy traffic on adjoining streets.

Grossmont
Harry Griffen Park

Description: One of San Diego's nicer parks with beautiful landscaping, PAR course, jogging path, sports fields and totlot.
Located at 9526 Milden Street, La Mesa
Transit service: No
Thomas Guide: Page 55, Grid F/5   Plentiful on-site parking
Open: Dawn to dusk   Jurisdiction: City of La Mesa   469-4128
Restrooms: Yes   Picnic tables/BBQs   Public telephone: No
Walking: Great for exercise walks in pleasant surroundings.

Grossmont
Northmont Park

Description: Five acres with jogger's track, totlot, PAR course.
Located at 6042 Severin Drive, La Mesa
Transit service: San Diego Trolley   Schedules: 231-8549
Thomas Guide: Page 55, Grid E/5   On-site parking
Open: 0600 to 2200   Jurisdiction: City of La Mesa   469-4128
Restrooms: Yes   Picnic tables/BBQs   Public telephone: No
Walks: Try the parkway and area surrounding this park.

Harbison Canyon
Old Ironsides County Park

Description: Community center, playground, ball court, creek.
Located on Harbison Canyon Road at Noakes Street, El Cajon
Transit service: CTS #888   Schedules: 233-3004
Thomas Guide: Page 58, Grid B/1   Street parking
Open: 24 Hours   Jurisdiction: County of San Diego   694-3049
Restrooms: Yes   Picnic area: Yes   Public telephone: No
Walks: The site is not suitable for exercise walking.

Harmony Grove
Avenida del Diablo Park

Description: A community park site of 12 undeveloped acres.
Located at 2300 Avenida del Diablo, Escondido
Transit service: NCTD #308, 382   Schedules: 722 or 743-6283
Thomas Guide: Page 22, Grid B/4   Street parking
Open: Closed   Jurisdiction: City of Escondido   741-4691
Restrooms: No   Picnic area: No   Public telephone: No
Walking: Closed to public use.

Imperial Beach
Border Field State Park

Description: Equestrian park adjacent to border with Mexico.
Located at the West end of Monument Road, Imperial Beach
Transit service: No
Thomas Guide: Page 73, Grid A/3   Limited on-site parking
Open: 0930 to 1800   Jurisdiction: State of California   435-5184
Restrooms: Yes   Picnic area: No   Public telephone: No
Walks: Marshland horse/hiking trails criss-cross the 680 acres.

Imperial Beach
Imperial Beach Sports Field

Description: Eight acres with playing fields, Teen Center, totlot.
Located at 400 Imperial Beach Boulevard, Imperial Beach
Transit service: MTS #933, #934   Schedules: 233-3004
Thomas Guide: Page 71, Grid A/5   On-site parking
Open: 0600 to 2200   Jurisdiction: City Imperial Beach   424-2277
Restrooms: Locked   Picnic tables/BBQs   Public telephone: Yes
Walks: There are paved parkways and a nice residential area.

Imperial Beach
Marina Vista Park

Description: Recreation building, gazebo, play fields and totlot.
Located at 800 Imperial Beach Boulevard, Imperial Beach
Transit service: MTS #933/934   Schedules: 233-3004
Thomas Guide: Page 71, Grid A/4   Street parking
Open: 0600 to 2200   Jurisdiction: City Imperial Beach   424-2277
Restrooms: Locked   Picnic tables/BBQs   Public telephone: No
Walks: Best on paved parkways and in the adjoining area.

Imperial Beach   Reama Park

Description: Mini-park with totlot, little shade but near beach.
Located at Elmwood Avenue and 2nd Street, Imperial Beach
Transit service: MTS #933   Schedules: 233-3004
Thomas Guide: Page 70-Z, Grid F/4   Street parking
Open: 0600 to 2200   Jurisdiction: City Imperial Beach   424-2277
Restrooms: No   Picnic tables: Yes   Public telephone: No
Walks: Nearby residential area and beach front would be best.

Imperial Beach   Sunset County Park

Description: An undeveloped County parksite for future growth.
Located at 1700 Sunset Avenue, San Diego
Transit service: No
Thomas Guide: Page 73, Grid C/1   Street parking
Open: No   Jurisdiction: County of San Diego   694-3049
Restrooms: No   Picnic area: No   Public telephone: No
Walks: Presently closed to public use.

Imperial Beach   Tijuana Estuary

Description: National wildlife refuge with educational exhibits.
Located at 301 Caspian Way, Imperial Beach
Transit service: MTS #901   Schedules: 233-3004
Thomas Guide: Page 70-Z, Grid F/5   On-site parking
Open: 0730 to 1600, Weekdays   Jurisdiction: State of California
Info: 575-1290   Restrooms: Yes   Picnic area: No   Telephone: Yes
Walks: Marked nature trails and in the nearby housing area.

Imperial Beach

Westview Park

Description: Playing field behind a housing area, next to school.
Located at 370 Calla Avenue, Imperial Beach
Transit service: No
Thomas Guide: Page 70-Z, Grid F/4   Street parking
Open: 0600 to 2200   Jurisdiction: City Imperial Beach 424-2277
Restrooms: No   Picnic area: No   Public telephone: No
Walks: The nearby residential area is recommended.

Jacumba

In-Ko-Pah County Park

Description: Park is closed. Desert overlook tower is open (Fee).
Located at 48686 Interstate 8, Jacumba
Transit service: CTS #888. #894   Schedules: 233-3004
Thomas Guide: Page 409, Grid F/5   Parking at tower only
Open: Park closed   Jurisdiction: County of S D   694-3049
Restrooms: At tower   Picnic area: No   Public telephone: No
Walks: The small Tower area is not suitable for long walks.

Jamacha

Steele Canyon County Park

Description: An undeveloped park site.
Located at 2925 Steele Canyon Road past Jamul Drive, Jamul
Transit service: No
Thomas Guide: Page 63-P, Grid A/5   Street parking
Open: Closed   Jurisdiction: County of San Diego   694-3049
Restrooms: No   Picnic area: No   Public telephone: No
Walks: Not open for public use.

Jesmond Dene

Jesmond Dene Park

Description: Playing fields, fitness course, baseball, on 37 acres.
Located at 2401 North Broadway, Escondido
Transit service: No
Thomas Guide: Page 17, Grid D/3   On-site parking
Open: Dawn to 2200   Jurisdiction: City of Escondido 741-4691
Restrooms: Yes   Picnic tables: Yes   Public telephone: No
Walking: Possible on non-used playing fields or random trails.

Park Walking in San Diego County

Julian   **Jess Martin County Park**

Description: Baseball complex, little shade over a small totlot.
Located at 2900 Cuyamaca Highway 79, Julian
Transit service: CTS #883, #884, #885   Schedules: 233-3004
Thomas Guide: Page 23-T, Grid D/3   On-site parking
Open: 24 Hours   Jurisdiction: County of San Diego   694-3049
Restrooms: Yes   Picnic area: No   Public telephone: No
Walks: Park is not suitable and the area lacks sidewalks.

Julian   **Julian County Park**

Description: Midget park, Museum and historic County library.
Located at 2811 Washington Street, Julian
Transit service: CTS #883, #884, #885   Schedules: 233-3004
Thomas Guide: Page 23-T, Grid C/3   Scarce street parking
Open: 24 Hours   Jurisdiction: County of San Diego   765-0227
Restrooms: Yes   Picnic tables: Yes   Public telephone: No
Walks: Park not suitable (too small) and no area sidewalks.

Julian   **William Heise Park**

Description: Camping and hot showers on 920 wooded acres.
Located at 4900 Heise Park Drive, Julian
Transit service: No
Thomas Guide: Page 23-T, Grid C/6   On-site parking fee
Open: Dawn to dusk   Jurisdiction: County of S D   565-3600
Restrooms: Yes   Picnic tables: Yes Public telephone: Yes
Walks: There is an excellent network of fine natural trails.

Kearney Mesa   **Kearney Mesa Community Park**

Description: A 71-acre park, pool, gym, shuffleboard and totlot.
Located at 3170 Armstrong Street, San Diego
Transit service: SDT #4   Schedules: 233-3004
Thomas Guide: Page 53, Grid B/3   Plentiful on-site parking
Open: 24 Hours   Jurisdiction: City of San Diego   573-1387
Restrooms: Yes   Picnic tables/BBQs Public telephone: Yes
Walking: Parkways plus Tecolate Canyon trails at the west end.

Kensington

Description: Neighborhood mini-park around a public library.
Located at 4121 Adams Avenue, San Diego
Transit service: SDT #11 Schedules: 233-3004
Thomas Guide: Page 61, Grid B/2 Limited street parking
Open: 24 Hours Jurisdiction: City of San Diego 236-6661
Restrooms: No Picnic tables: Yes Public telephone: No
Walks: Park has no paths. Residential area walking is possible.

La Costa

Cadencia Park

Description: Baseball, play field and totlot on two acres.
Located at 3310 Cadencia Street, Carlsbad
Transit service: No
Thomas Guide: Page 20, Grid C/6 Street parking
Open:24 Hours Jurisdiction: City of Carlsbad 434-2839
Restrooms: No Picnic area: No Public telephone: No
Walks: The attractive nearby residential area is suitable.

La Costa

La Costa Canyon Park

Description: Three acres, tennis, ball courts, horseshoes, totlot.
Located at Pueblo Street and Rana Court, Carlsbad
Transit service: No
Thomas Guide: Page 20, Grid C/6 Street parking
Open: 24 Hours Jurisdiction: City of Carlsbad 434-2836
Restrooms: Yes Picnic tables/BBQs Public telephone: No
Walks: A pleasant park with a surrounding area for walking.

La Costa　　　　　　　　　　**La Costa Meadows Park**

Description: About four acres of neighborhood park with playing
fields and totlot next to a school. Also known as Fuerte Park.
Located at 6989 El Fuerte Street, Carlsbad
Transit service: No
Thomas Guide: Page 20, Grid C/4　　　　　　On-site parking
Open: 24 Hours　　Jurisdiction: City of Carlsbad　　434-2836
Restrooms: No　　Picnic area: No　　Public telephone: No
Walking: Best in nearby residential area, adjoining hillsides.

La Jolla　　　　　　　　　　**Bird Rock Park**

Description: Playing fields shared with elementary school.
Located on Bellevue Place, La Jolla
Transit service: SDT #30, #34　　　　　Schedules: 233-3004
Thomas Guide: Page 43-A, Grid F/5　　Limited street parking
Open: 24 Hours　　Jurisdiction: City of San Diego　　236-661
Restrooms: No　　Picnic area: No　　　Public telephone: No
Walks: Not recommended.

La Jolla　　　　　　　　　　**Cliffridge Park**

Description: Baseball playing fields, playground and totlot.
Located at 8311 Cliffridge Avenue, La Jolla
Transit service: No
Thomas Guide: Page 44, Grid B/3　　　　　Street parking
Open: 24 Hours　　Jurisdiction: City of San Diego　　236-6661
Restrooms: Yes　　Picnic area: No　　Public telephone: No
Walks: Not suitable due to heavy ballfield activity.

La Jolla　　　　　　　　　　**La Jolla Athletic Area**

Description: Known as Allen Field, an expanse of playing fields.
Located at 8908 Torrey Pines Road, La Jolla
Transit service: SDT #30, #34, #41　　　　Schedules: 233-3004
Thomas Guide: Page 44, Grid B/2　　Limited on-site parking
Open: 24 Hours　　Jurisdiction: City of San Diego　　236-6661
Restrooms: Yes　　Picnic area: No　　Public telephone: No
Walks: Excellent, when play fields are not in use.

La Jolla — La Jolla Park and Recreation Center

Description: Central area with tennis, ball courts, fields, totlot.
Located at 615 Prospect Street, La Jolla
Transit service: SDT #34 — Schedules: 233-3004
Thomas Guide: Page 43-A, Grid E/2 — On-site parking
Open: 0700 to 2100 — Jurisdiction: City of San Diego — 454-2071
Restrooms: Yes — Picnic area: Small — Public telephone: Yes
Walks: Not suitable due to adjoining business-area congestion.

La Jolla — Mata Park

Description: Tiny strip of grass covering a pumping station.
Located at 2211 Avenida de la Playa, La Jolla
Transit service: SDT #34 — Schedules: 233-3004
Thomas Guide: Page 44, Grid A/4 — Street parking
Open: 24 Hours — Jurisdiction: City of San Diego — 236-6661
Restrooms: No — Picnic area: No — Public telephone: Nearby
Walks: In the surrounding upscale business district.

La Jolla — Pottery Canyon Park

Description: Small hikers park with narrow entry drive.
Located at 2737 Torrey Pines Road, La Jolla
Transit service: No
Thomas Guide: Page 44, Grid B/4 — Very limited on-site parking
Open: 0800 to 1800 Hours — Jurisdiction: City of S D — 236-6661
Restrooms: No — Picnic area: No — Public telephone: No
Walks: There is a half-mile hiking trail through natural terrain.

La Jolla   **Soledad Park**

Description: Mountain top park, superb view in every direction.
Located at 7000 La Jolla Scenic Drive South, La Jolla
Transit service: No
Thomas Guide: Page 44, Grid B/5   Plentiful on-site parking
Open: 24 Hours   Jurisdiction: City of San Diego   236-6661
Restrooms: No   Picnic area: No   Public telephone: No
Walks: Limited size of the mountain top is not suitable.

La Jolla   **Starkey Mini-Park**

Description: Small and lovely hillside neighborhood park.
Located at 6707 Draper Avenue, La Jolla
Transit service: SDT #30, #34   Schedules: 233-3004
Thomas Guide: Page 43-A, Grid E/3   Street parking
Open: 24 Hours   Jurisdiction: City of San Diego   236-6661
Restrooms: No   Picnic tables: Yes   Public telephone: No
Walks: Use the short parkway, hillsides and area sidewalks.

La Jolla   **Union Place Circle Park**

Description: The grassed center of a traffic circle.
At joining of Park Row, Park Row and Park Row, La Jolla
Transit service: SDT #30, #34   Schedules: 233-3004
Thomas Guide: Page 43-A, Grid F/2   Street parking
Open: 24 Hours   Jurisdiction: City of San Diego   236-6661
Restrooms: No   Picnic area: No   Public telephone: No
Walks: In the surrounding residential area.

La Jolla   **Via Del Norte Park**

Description: Mini-mini park with adjoining bicycle trail.
Located at 407 Via Del Norte, La Jolla
Transit service: SDT #30, #34   Schedules: 233-3004
Thomas Guide: Page 43-A, Grid E/4   Street parking
Open: 24 Hours   Jurisdiction: City of San Diego   236-6661
Restrooms: No   Picnic area: No   Public telephone: No
Walks: Park is too small. Nearby residential area is walkable.

La Jolla

Villa La Jolla Park

Description: Grassed neighborhood playfield and totlot.
Located at 8371 Via Mallorca, La Jolla
Transit service: SDT #34-A, #150 Schedules: 233-3004
Thomas Guide: Page 44, Grid C/3 Street parking
Open: 24 Hours Jurisdiction: City of San Diego 236-6611
Restrooms: No Picnic tables: Yes Public telephone: No
Walks: There is a paved loop parkway and a nice nearby area.

Lake Henshaw

Lake Henshaw Park

Description: Fishing, camping, play area in private park.
Located at 26439 Highway 76 (Lake Henshaw), Santa Ysabel
Transit service: No (This is a private lake resort)
Thomas Guide: Page 401, Grid C/4-5 On-site parking fee
Open: 24-Hours. Jurisdiction: Lake Henshaw Resort 782-3501
Restrooms: Yes Picnic tables: Yes Public telephone: Yes
Walks: There are lake-front trails and paths in the site.

Lake Henshaw

San Luis Rey Picnic Area

Description: Lovely forested valley with picnic facilities.
Located on South side of Highway 76, west of Lake Henshaw
Transit service: No (Large highway signs)
Thomas Guide: Page 401, Grid B/4 On-site parking
Open: 0800 to 2000 Jurisdiction: U.S.Forest Service 782-3472
Restrooms: Yes Picnic tables/BBQs Public telephone: No
Walks: There are posted driveways and maintained trails.

Lake Murray

Lake Murray

Description: Ballfields, tennis, playgrounds and access to trails.
Located at 7001 Lake Murray Drive, San Diego
Transit service: SDT #115 Schedules: 233-3004
Thomas Guide: Page 55, Grid A/5 Plentiful on-site parking
Open: 0600 to 2000 Jurisdiction: City of San Diego 236-6631
Restrooms: Yes Picnic tables: Yes Public telephone: No
Walking: Obtain directions to Mission Trails, Cowles Mountain.

Lakeside   Cactus County Park

Description: Ballfields and outbuildings on 84-acre ranch site.
Located at 10610 Ashwood Street, Lakeside
Transit service: No
Thomas Guide: Page 48, Grid F/2   On-site parking
Open: ????   Jurisdiction: County of San Diego   694-3049
Restrooms: Yes   Picnic area: No   Public telephone: No
Walks: Neither park nor area are suitable for exercise walking.

Lakeside   El Capitan Open Space Preserve

Description: 2800 Primitive acres and miles of trails/roads.
Located at 13775 Blue Sky Ranch Road, Lakeside
Transit service: No
Thomas Guide: Page 42-P, Grid D/2   Limited on-site parking
Open: 0800 to dusk Jurisdiction: County of San Diego 694-3049
Restrooms: No   Picnic area: No   Public telephone: No
Walks: Use the developed mine roads and random trails.

Lakeside   El Monte County Park

Description: Ballfields, horseshoe pits, playground and totlot.
Located at 15835 El Monte Road, Lakeside
Transit service: No
Thomas Guide: Page 405, Grid A/6   On-site parking fee
Open: 0930 to 1900 Jurisdiction: County of San Diego 694-3049
Restrooms: Yes   Picnic area: Yes   Public telephone: No
Walks: Park area and surrounding hillsides are excellent.

Lakeside

Lake Jennings Park

Description: Fishing, hiking, camping, playgrounds and totlot.
Located on Bass Drive, Lakeside
Transit service: CTS #864   Schedules: 233-3004
Thomas Guide: Page 49, Grid C/3   On-site parking fee
Open: Dawn to dusk   Jurisdiction: County of S D   694-3049
Restrooms: Yes   Picnic tables/BBQs   Public telephone: Yes
Walks: Parkways and many natural trails in 100-acre site.

Lakeside

Lakeside County Park

Description: This is a portion of the El Capitan Preserve.
Located on Pata Ranch Road off Wildcat Canyon Road, Lakeside
Transit service: No
Thomas Guide: Page 42-P, Grid E/4   Limited on-site parking
Open: 0800 to 1900 Jurisdiction: County of San Diego 694-3049
Restrooms: No   Picnic area: No   Public telephone: No
Walks: There are random natural trails for experienced hikers.

Lakeside

Lindo Lake County Park

Description: Lake, ballfields, horseshoes, tennis and totlot.
Located at 9851 Vine Street, Lakeside
Transit service: CTS #848, #854   Schedules: 233-3004
Thomas Guide: Page 48, Grid F/3   On-site parking
Open: 24 Hours   Jurisdiction: County of San Diego   694-3049
Restrooms: Yes   Picnic tables/BBQs   Public telephone: Yes
Walks: 55-Acre urban site, parkways and path around the lake.

Lakeside
Oak Oasis County Park

Description: A nature study preserve and hiking trails park.
Located on Wildcat Canyon Road near Blue Sky Ranch Road
Transit service: No
Thomas Guide: Page 42-P, Grid B/2
Open: By request   Jurisdiction: County of San Diego   694-3049
Restrooms: Yes   Picnic area: No   Public telephone: No
Walks: Only open to organized groups by special reservation.

Lake Sutherland
Sutherland Reservoir

Description: Water Utilities storage providing limited park use.
Located at north end of Sutherland Rd. off Highway 78, Ramona
Transit service: No
Thomas Guide: Page 405, Grid B/l   On-site parking
Open: Sat and Sun   Jurisdiction: City of San Diego   465-3474
Restrooms: Yes   Picnic area: Yes   Public telephone: Yes
Walks: There are a number of natural hiking trails in the area.

Lake Wohlford
Lake Wohlford Picnic Area

Description: Regional park with 1100 acres of natural terrain
around a large lake. Village store nearby. Boats and fishing.
Located at 25453 Lake Wohlford Road, Escondido
Transit service: No
Thomas Guide: Page 18, Grid E/3   On-site parking fee
Open: Dawn to dusk   Jurisdiction: City of Escondido   749-2661
Restrooms: Yes   Picnic tables/BBQs   Public telephone: Yes
Walking: Lake perimeter path, random trails, fire roads in area.

La Mesa
Aztec Park

Description: A nice four-acre turfed playground with totlot.
Located at Aztec Drive and Morocco Drive, La Mesa
Transit service: CTS #854   Schedules: 233-3004
Thomas Guide: Page 55, Grid C/6   Street parking
Open: 0600 to 2100   Jurisdiction: City of La Mesa   469-4128
Restrooms: Yes   Picnic tables/BBQs   Public telephone: No
Walks: Area walking is suggested as paved parkway is short.

La Mesa   Collier Park

Description: Beautifully landscaped eight acres with nice shade trees; tennis, playground and totlot.
Located at 4401 Palm Avenue, La Mesa
Transit service: CTS #854, S D Trolley   Schedules: 233-3004
Thomas Guide: Page 62, Grid D/2   Limited on-site parking
Open: 0600 to 2200   Jurisdiction: City of La Mesa   469-4128
Restrooms: Yes   Picnic tables/BBQs   Public telephone: No
Walks: There are no parkways and area traffic is heavy.

La Mesa   Damon Lane County Park

Description: Large grassed field with cluster of shade trees.
Located on Damon Lane near Zoldero Road, La Mesa
Transit service: No
Thomas Guide: Page 63, Grid D/3   Street parking
Open: 24 Hours   Jurisdiction: County of San Diego   694-3049
Restrooms: No   Picnic area: No   Public telephone: No
Walks: Parkland only. There are no area sidewalks.

La Mesa   Highwood Park

Description: Sloping eight acres, tennis, ball courts and totlot.
Located at 4200 Parks Avenue, La Mesa
Transit service: SDT #7   Schedules: 233-3004
Thomas Guide: Page 62, Grid; C/3   On-site parking
Open: 0600 to 2200   Jurisdiction: City of La Mesa   469-4128
Restrooms: Yes   Picnic tables/BBQs   Public telephone: No
Walks: There is a short parkway but no area sidewalks.

La Mesa   Jackson Park

Description: Totlot and play area on neighborhood four acres.
Located at Jackson and Laird Streets, La Mesa
Transit service: SDT #81   Schedules: 233-3004
Thomas Guide: Page 55, Grid C-D/5   Street parking
Open: 0600 to 2200   Jurisdiction: City of La Mesa   469-4128
Restrooms: Yes   Picnic tables: Yes   Public telephone: No
Walks: Park site is suitable for exercise walking.

Park Walking in San Diego County

La Mesa

Description: Ten acres with ball court, tennis, horseshoes, totlot.
Located at 8951 Dallas Street, La Mesa
Transit service: No
Thomas Guide: Page 55, Grid E/5 Adequate on-site parking
Open: 0600 to 2200 Jurisdiction: City of La Mesa 469-4128
Restrooms: Yes Picnic tables/BBQs Public Telephone: No
Walks: There is a good selection of paved parkways for walking.

La Mesa

Mac Arthur Park

Description: A large facility with recreation center, public pool,
golf, baseball fields, playground and totlot.
Located at University Avenue and Memorial Drive, La Mesa
Transit service: SDT #7, #15, CTS #854 Schedules: 233-3004
Thomas Guide: Page 62, Grid D/1 On-site parking
Open: 0600 to 2200 Jurisdiction: City of La Mesa 469-4128
Restrooms: Yes Picnic tables/BBQs Public telephone: No
Walks: The parksite has many opportunities for exercise walks.

La Mesa

Porter Park

Description: A senior center with shuffleboard courts.
Located at 8425 University Avenue, La Mesa
Transit service: SDT #7 Schedules: 233-3004
Thomas Guide: Page 62, Grid D/1 Limited on-site parking
Open: 0600 to 2200 Jurisdiction: City of La Mesa 469-4128
Restrooms: Yes Picnic tables: Yes Public telephone: Yes
Walks: The surrounding area sidewalks would be useful.

La Mesa Rolando Park

Description: Well kept baseball field complex with a totlot.
Located at 6610 Vigo Drive, La Mesa
Transit service: SDT #7   Schedules: 233-3004
Thomas Guide: Page 62, Grid A/2   On-site parking
Open: 0600 to 2200   Jurisdiction: City of La Mesa   469-4128
Restrooms: Yes   Picnic tables/BBQs   Public telephone: No
Walks: Neither park nor area are best for exercise walking.

La Mesa Sunset Park

Description: Seven acres, fitness center, playfields and totlot.
Located at 5540 Lake Park Way, La Mesa
Transit service: SDT #81   Schedules: 233-3004
Thomas Guide: Page 55, Grid B/5   Unpaved on-site parking
Open: 0600 to 2200   Jurisdiction: City of La Mesa   469-4128
Restrooms: Yes   Picnic tables/BBQs   Public Telephone: No
Walks: Use park site only as adjacent streets are unpaved.

La Mesa Sunshine Park

Description: A two-acre grassed sports and play field.
Located at 70th Street and Bruce Court, La Mesa
Transit service: No
Thomas Guide: Page 62, Grid A/2   Street parking
Open: 0600 to 2200   Jurisdiction: City of La Mesa   469-4128
Restrooms: Yes   Picnic tables/BBQs   Public telephone: No
Walks: There is limited walking potential in this parksite.

La Mesa Vista La Mesa Park

Description: Little League, play area and totlot on three acres.
Located at Hoffman Avenue and King Street, La Mesa
Transit service: No
Thomas Guide: Page 62, Grid A/3   On-site parking
Open: 0600 to 2200   Jurisdiction: City of La Mesa   469-4128
Restrooms: Yes   Picnic area: No   Public telephone: No
Walks: Parksite walkable when baseball field is not in use.

La Presa
Spring Valley County Park

Description: Play fields, horseshoe pits and totlot on six acres.
Located on Jamacha Boulevard at Gillespie Drive, Spring Valley
Transit service: CTS #856, SDT #11, #36   Schedules: 233-3004
Thomas Guide: Page 67, Grid D/2   On-site parking
Open: 0800 to 1700; 2000 Sat-Sun   Jurisdiction: County of S D
Information: 694-3049   Restrooms: Yes   Picnic tables: Yes
Telephone: No   Walks: Not recommended, heavy traffic in area.

La Presa
Sweetwater Lane County Park

Description: Partially grassed playing field and park site.
Located at 1400 Sweetwater Lane, Spring Valley
Transit service: No
Thomas Guide: Page 67, Grid E/1   Street parking
Open: 24 Hours   Jurisdiction: County of San Diego   694-3049
Restrooms: No   Picnic area: No   Public telephone: No
Walks: Parksite not suitable and area streets are unpaved.

Lemon Grove
Lemon Grove Park

Description: Neighborhood park, shade trees, playground, totlot.
Located at 2285 Washington Street, Lemon Grove
Transit service: SDT #36   Schedules: 233-3004
Thomas Guide: Page 62, Grid C/5   On-site parking
Open: Dawn to dusk   Jurisdiction: City Lemon Grove 668-4575
Restrooms: Yes   Picnic tables/BBQs   Public telephone: No
Walks: There are no parkways or nearby area sidewalks.

Lemon Grove

Mount Vernon Park

Description: Area playground with gazebos, shade trees, totlot.
Located at 7995 Mount Vernon Street, Lemon Grove
Transit service: SDT #36   Schedules: 233-3004
Thomas Guide: Page 62, Grid A/5   On-site parking
Open: Dawn to dusk   Jurisdiction: City Lemon Grove 668-4575
Restrooms: Yes   Picnic tables/BBQs   Public telephone: No
Walks: Grass parkland only. No area sidewalks.

Leucadia

Leucadia Roadside Park

Description: The County's smallest park for a shaded lunch.
Located at 800 Old Highway 101, Encinitas
Transit service: NCTD #301, #361   Schedules: 722 or 743-6283
Thomas Guide: Page 24, Grid D/2   Limited curb-side parking
Open: Dawn to dusk   Jurisdiction: City of Encinitas   944-3380
Restrooms: No   Picnic tables: Yes   Public telephone: Nearby
Walks: No room to walk in the park, fast traffic surrounding.

Lincoln Acres

Lincoln Acres Park

Description: Community center, playground, totlot, ball court.
Located at Granger Avenue and Chaffee Street, National City
Transit service: No
Thomas Guide: Page 69, Grid E/1   Street Parking
Open: 24 Hours   Jurisdiction: County of San Diego   694-3049
Restrooms: No   Picnic area: Yes   Public telephone: No
Walks: Exercise walking feasible in the nearby area.

Park Walking in San Diego County

Linda Vista   Kelly Street Park

Description: Small neighborhood park with playground.
Located at 6640 Kelly Street, San Diego
Transit service: SDT #4, #25   Schedules: 233-3004
Thomas Guide: Page 53, Grid B/5   Scarce street parking
Open: 24 Hours   Jurisdiction: City of San Diego   236-6661
Restrooms: Yes   Picnic tables: Yes   Public telephone: No
Walks: Paved loop parkway only. Area walks not feasible.

Linda Vista   Linda Vista Community Park

Description: Recreation building, play fields, tennis, ball courts.
Located at 7064 Levant Street, San Diego
Transit service: SDT #4, #25, #41   Schedules: 233-3004
Thomas Guide: Page 53, Grid B/4   On-site parking
Open: 24 Hours   Jurisdiction: City of San Diego   573-1392
Restrooms: Yes   Picnic area: Yes   Public telephone: No
Walks: Parksite only. Area traffic is congested and fast.

Linda Vista   Tecolate Canyon Natural Park

Description: Entrance to canyon from Linda Vista Park.
Located at 7064 Levant Street, San Diego
Transit service: SDT #4, #25, #41   Schedules: 233-3004
Thomas Guide: Page 53, Grid A & B/2-6   On-site parking
Open: 24 Hours   Jurisdiction: City of San Diego   236-6661
Restrooms: No   Picnic area: No   Public telephone: No
Walks: The canyon is an excellent location for moderate hiking.

Logan Heights   Chicano Park

Description: Magnificent Hispanic art on Bay bridge supports.
Located at 1982 National Avenue, San Diego
Transit service: SDT #11   Schedules: 233-3004
Thomas Guide: Page 65, Grid D/3   Scarce street parking
Open: 24 Hours   Jurisdiction: City of San Diego   236-6661
Restrooms: Yes   Picnic area: No   Public telephone: No
Walks: This is an industrial area. Walks are not feasible.

Logan Heights

Clay Avenue Mini-Park

Description: Small landscaped parcel equipped with a totlot.
Located at 3157 Clay Avenue, San Diego
Transit service: SDT #3. #4, S D Trolley   Schedules: 233-3004
Thomas Guide: Page 65, Grid F/3   Street parking
Open: 24 Hours   Jurisdiction: City of San Diego   236-6661
Restrooms: No   Picnic area: No   Public telephone: No
Walks: Not suitable due to size and area traffic congestion.

Logan Heights

41st Street Mini-Park

Description: Landscaped corner Mini-Park with a totlot.
Located at 4105 Gamma Street, San Diego
Transit service: SDT #13   Schedules: 233-3004
Thomas Guide: Page 66, Grid B/4   Street parking
Open: 24 Hours   Jurisdiction: City of San Diego   236-6661
Restrooms: No   Picnic tables: Yes   Public telephone: No
Walks: Not recommended due to fast traffic on nearby streets.

Logan Heights

John F. Kennedy Park

Description: Neighborhood park with play fields and totlot.
Located at 4825 Ocean View Boulevard, San Diego
Transit service: SDT #3, #4, #13   Schedules: 233-3004
Thomas Guide: Page 66, Grid C/3   Street parking
Open: 24 Hours   Jurisdiction: City of San Diego   236-6661
Restrooms: Yes   Picnic tables: Yes   Public telephone: No
Walks: Use parkways only, as nearby streets are narrow.

Logan Heights   Memorial Park

Description: Recreation center, large park, playground, totlot.
Located at 2902 Marcy Avenue, San Diego
Transit service: SDT #3, #11   Schedules: 233-3004
Thomas Guide: Page 65, Grid F/3   Limited on-site parking
Open: 24 Hours   Jurisdiction: City of San Diego   232-5210
Restrooms: Yes   Picnic tables/BBQs   Public telephone: No
Walks: Grassed parkland only. Area traffic moves rapidly.

Logan Heights   Mountain View Park

Description: Playground, ball court, gazebo, tennis and totlot.
Located at 551 South 40th Street, San Diego
Transit service: SDT #3   Schedules: 233-3004
Thomas Guide: Page 66, Grid B/3   On-site parking
Open: 24 Hours   Jurisdiction: City of San Diego   264-6095
Restrooms: Yes   Picnic tables: Yes   Public telephone: No
Walks: The many paved parkways are excellent.

Logan Heights   Southcrest Park

Description: Senior center, weight/crafts room, ball fields, tennis
and shuffleboard in a large neighborhood park complex.
Located at 4149 Newton Avenue, San Diego
Transit service: SDT #11, #13   Schedules: 233-3004
Thomas Guide: Page 66, Grid B/4   On-site parking
Open: 24 Hours   Jurisdiction: City of San Diego   264-6108
Restrooms: Yes   Picnic tables/BBQs   Public telephone: No
Walks: Paved parkways are recommended for exercise walking.

Logan Heights   Southeast Sports Field

Description: Baseball and ball courts in an 18-acre facility.
Located at 1035 South 45th Street, San Diego
Transit service: SDT #11,#13   Schedules: 233-3004
Thomas Guide: Page 66, Grid C/4   On-site parking
Open: 24 Hours   Jurisdiction: City of San Diego   264-0584
Restrooms: Yes   Picnic tables: Yes   Public telephone: No
Walks: Use of parkways is recommended for exercise walking.

Park Walking in San Diego County

Logan Heights   **30th Street Mini-Park**

Description: Small neighborhood play area on a residential lot.
Located at 702 South 30th Street, San Diego
Transit service: SDT #3, #11   Schedules: 233-3004
Thomas Guide: Page 65, Grid F/3   Street parking
Open: 24 Hours   Jurisdiction: City of San Diego   236-6661
Restrooms: No   Picnic area: No   Public telephone: No
Walks: Park is too small for walking, streets are traffic heavy.

Loma Portal   **Plumosa Park**

Description: Grass playing field in upscale residential district.
Located at Plumosa Drive and Chatsworth Blvd, San Diego
Transit service: SDT #35   Schedules: 233-3004
Thomas Guide: Page 59, Grid D/4   Street parking
Open: 24 Hours   Jurisdiction: City of San Diego   236-6661
Restrooms: No   Picnic area: No   Public telephone: No
Walks: Area residential walking only. Park slopes not suitable.

Lower Otay Reservoir   **Lower Otay County Park**

Description: Day use camping, fishing, playgrounds and totlot.
Located at Wueste Road and Park Drive
Transit service: No   (Site also known as Otay Lake Park)
Thomas Guide: Page 72-N, Grid E/2   On-site parking fee
Open: Dawn to dusk   Jurisdiction: County of S D   694-3049
Restrooms: Yes   Picnic area: Yes   Public telephone: Yes
Walks: An excellent park for trail-hiking exercise.

Lower Otay Reservoir   **Otay County Park**

Description: A vast expanse of natural land below Otay dam.
Located on Wueste Road and Park Drive, San Diego
Transit service: No
Thomas Guide: Page 72-N, Grid F/2   On-site parking
Open: Reservation only   Jurisdiction: County of S D   694-3049
Restrooms: No   Picnic area: No   Public telephone: No
Walks: This is a caravan camping area with some nature trails.

Lower Otay Reservoir

Recreation Station

Description: Camping, fishing, boating and hiking facility.
Located at Wueste Road and Park Drive
Transit service: No   Jurisdiction: City of San Diego
Thomas Guide: Page 72-N. Grid E/2   On-site parking
Open: Dawn to dusk, Wednesday, Saturday, Sunday
Information: 465-3474   Restrooms: Yes   Picnic area: Yes
Telephone: Yes Walks: Wide selection of random natural trails.

Lynwood Hills

Halecrest Park

Description: Hillside Mini-Park, totlot, shade trees, ocean view.
Located at 421 East "J" Street, Chula Vista
Transit service: No
Thomas Guide: Page 70, Grid A/4   Limited on-site parking
Open: 0600 to 2230 Jurisdiction: City of Chula Vista 691-5071
Restrooms: No   Picnic tables/BBQs   Public telephone: No
Walks: Best opportunities are in the adjoining areas.

Lynwood Hills

Paseo del Rey Park

Description: Lovely, partially natural, playground and totlot.
Located at 750 Paseo del Rey, Chula Vista
Transit service: CVT #704   Schedules: 233-3004
Thomas Guide: Page 70, Grid B/5   Street parking
Open: 0700 to 2230 Jurisdiction: City of Chula Vista 691-5071
Restrooms: No   Picnic tables/BBQs   Public Telephone: No
Walks: Use the short parkways and nearby undeveloped area.

Lynwood Hills

Sunridge Park

Description: Neighborhood park, playground and totlot.
Located at 860 East "J" Street, Chula Vista
Transit service: CVT #707   Schedules: 233-3004
Thomas Guide: Page 70, Grid C/5   Street parking
Open: 0700 to 2230 Jurisdiction: City of Chula Vista 691-5071
Restrooms: No   Picnic tables: Yes   Public telephone: No
Walks: Paved parkways and nearby residential area are best.

Lynwood Hills

Description: New neighborhood playground with playfields, ball fields, a PAR course and totlot.
Located at 450 Hidden Vista, Chula Vista
Transit service: CVT #705A　　　　　　Schedules: 233-3004
Thomas Guide: Page 70, Grid B/3　　　　　　Street parking
Open: 0700 to 2230　Jurisdiction: City of Chula Vista　691-5071
Restrooms: Yes　　Picnic tables: Yes　　Public telephone: No
Walks: No parkways but nearby area is pleasant for walking.

McCain Valley

Description: Remote desert park for camping under shade trees.
Located 13 miles from I-8 on McCain Valley Road, Boulevard
Transit service: No　　　　　　(This is an unpaved road)
Thomas Guide: Page 409, Grid D/3　　　　　On-site parking
Open: 24 Hours　　Jurisdiction: U.S. Bureau Land Management
Information: 352-5842　　Restrooms: Yes　Picnic area: Yes
Telephone: No　Walks: Wide selection of informal desert paths.

McCain Valley   Lark Canyon

Description: Motorcycle and ORV play area and public campsite.
Located 7.5 miles from I-8 on McCain Valley Road, Boulevard
Transit service: No   (This is an unpaved road)
Thomas Guide: Page 409, Grid D/4   On-site parking
Open: 24 Hours   Jurisdiction: U.S. Bureau Land Management
Information: 352-5842   Restrooms: Yes   Picnic area: Yes
Telephone: No   Walks: Dangerous due to intense vehicle activity

Middle Town   Balboa Park

Description: The 1200-acre crown jewel of all SD area parks.
Museums, superb zoo and miles of fine parkways. A must!
Located off the Cabrillo Freeway on marked exits.
Transit service: SDT #7, #16,   Schedules: 233-3004
Thomas Guide: Page 60, Grid D/5   On-site parking
Open: 24 Hours   Jurisdiction: City of San Diego   525-8200
Restrooms: Yes   Picnic areas: Many   Public telephone: Yes
Walking: The Information Office has free maps of the parksite.

Middle Town   King Promenade

Description: Future (1994) Trolley park near Seaport Village.
Located along Harbor Drive between "G" and Fifth, San Diego
Transit service: San Diego Trolley   Schedules: 231-8549
Thomas Guide: Page H, Grid B-C/6   Area parking available
Open: 1984   Jurisdiction: Centre City Development   235-2222
Restrooms: Yes   Picnic area: No   Public telephone: Yes
Walks: A serpentine walk is planned for the twelve-acre strip.

Middle Town   Morley Field Recreation Center

Description: Bicycle track, ballfield, tennis, pool, archery, boccie.
Located at 2221 Morley Field Drive, San Diego
Transit service: SDT #2   Schedules: 233-3004
Thomas Guide: Page 60, Grid E/5   On-site parking
Open: 24 Hours   Jurisdiction: City of San Diego   298-0920
Restrooms: Yes   Picnic area: Yes   Public telephone: Yes
Walks: Ask about nature trails and guided Balboa Park walks.

Middle Town   Pantoja Park

Description: Center city park with benches and shade trees.
Located at 524 "G" Street, San Diego
Transit service: All "Downtown" routes   Schedules: 233-3004
Thomas Guide: Page 65, Grid C/1   Metered street parking
Open: 24 Hours   Jurisdiction: City of San Diego   236-6661
Restrooms: No   Picnic area: No   Telephone: No
Walks: Parkways and the interesting nearby Gaslamp Quarter.

Middle Town   William Davis Health House and Park

Description: Tiny landscaped corner park and historical house.
Located at Fourth Avenue and Island Street, San Diego
Transit service: All "Downtown" routes   Schedules: 233-3004
Thomas Guide: Page 65, Grid C/2   Metered street parking
Open: 0800 to 1700   Jurisdiction: City of San Diego   236-6661
Restrooms: No   Picnic area: No   Telephone: No
Walks: Site is a feature of the downtown Gaslamp Quarter.

Mira Mesa   Canyonside Community Park

Description: Ballfields, tennis, playgrounds, totlot, playgrounds.
Located at 12350 Black Mountain Road, San Diego
Transit service: No
Thomas Guide: Page 35, Grid F/5   On-site parking
Open: 24 Hours   Jurisdiction: City of San Diego   538-8131
Restrooms: Yes   Picnic tables/BBQs   Public telephone: Yes
Walks: Walking opportunities include numerous canyon trails.

Mira Mesa   El Camino Memorial Park

Description: This is a privately owned cemetery.
Located at 5600 Carroll Canyon Road, San Diego
Transit service: No
Thomas Guide: Page 39, Grid B/4
Open: Inquire   Jurisdiction: Private ownership   453-2121
Restrooms: No   Picnic area: No   Public telephone: No
Walks: No

Mira Mesa   Los Penasquitos Canyon Preserve

Description: 2240 Acres in suburban San Diego with hiking and
equestrian trails, waterfall and historic adobe.
Located at 12300 Black Mountain Road, San Diego
Transit service: No
Thomas Guide: Page 35, Grid F/5   On-site parking
Open: 0800 to dusk   Jurisdiction: City/County of SD   236-6661
Restrooms: Yes   Picnic area: Yes   Public telephone: Yes
Walks: Miles of great walking trails and random paths.

Mira Mesa   Maddox Park

Description: Small neighborhood park, PAR course and totlot.
Located on Flanders Drive at Dabney Drive, San Diego
Transit service: SDT DART   Schedules: 293-3278
Thomas Guide: Page 39, Grid D/3   Street parking
Open: 24 Hours   Jurisdiction: City of San Diego   236-6661
Restrooms: No   Picnic tables/BBQs   Public telephone: No
Walks: Area residential walking is recommended.

Mira Mesa   Mesa Verde Park

Description: Neighborhood park, grassed play field and totlot.
Located at 8350 Gold Coast Drive, San Diego
Transit service: SDT #30, SDT DART   Schedules: 233-3004
Thomas Guide: Page 39, Grid E/3   Street parking
Open: 24 Hours   Jurisdiction: City of San Diego   236-6661
Restrooms: Yes   Picnic tables: Yes   Public telephone: No
Walks: The best walking ventures will be in the park site.

Mira Mesa   Mesa Viking Park

Description: Neighborhood site, playground equipment, totlot.
Located at 11170 Westonhill Drive, San Diego
Transit service: No
Thomas Guide: Page 39, Grid F/1   Street parking
Open: 24 Hours   Jurisdiction: City of San Diego   236-6661
Restrooms: No   Picnic tables: Yes   Public telephone: No
Walks: Try the paved parkways and pleasant nearby areas.

Mira Mesa   Mira Mesa Park

Description: Rec center, ball courts, playground, totlot, 18-acres.
Located at 8575 New Salem Street, San Diego
Transit service: SDT #30   Schedules: 233-3004
Thomas Guide: Page 39, Grid E/2   On-site parking
Open: 24 Hours   Jurisdiction: City of San Diego   566-5141
Restrooms: Yes   Picnic tables: Yes   Public telephone: Yes
Walks: On-site parkways and nearby areas are recommended.

Mira Mesa   **Winterwood Community Park**

Description: Dual-level neighborhood park with totlot.
Located at 7540 Winterwood Lane, San Diego
Transit service: SDT DART   Schedules: 293-3278
Thomas Guide: Page 39, Grid C/2   Limited street parking
Open: 24 Hours   Jurisdiction: City of San Diego   236-6661
Restrooms: No   Picnic tables: Yes   Public telephone: No
Walks: Use both on-site paved parkways and the nearby area.

Mission Bay   **Dana Landing**

Description: A bay-side park area and boat launching facility.
Located on Dana Landing Road, San Diego
Transit service: SDT #81   Schedules: 233-3004
Thomas Guide: Page 59, Grid C/2   On-site parking
Open: 24 Hours   Jurisdiction: City of San Diego   236-6661
Restrooms: Yes   Picnic area: No   Public telephone: Yes
Walks: The area is busy with boat handling.

Mission Bay   **Fiesta Island**

Description: A flat island; camping, playfields and sports use.
Located on Fiesta Island Road, San Diego
Transit service: No
Thomas Guide: Page 59, Grid D/1   Plentiful on-site parking
Open: 24 Hours   Jurisdiction: City of San Diego   236-6661
Restrooms: Yes   Picnic area: Yes   Public telephone: No
Walks: There is an excellent loop parkway and many trails.

Mission Bay   Hospitality Point

Description: Small park on point of land in Mission Bay.
Located at 2500 Quivira Way, San Diego
Transit service: No
Thomas Guide: Page 59, Grid B/2   On-site parking
Open: 24 Hours   Jurisdiction: City of San Diego   236-6661
Restrooms: Yes   Picnic area: Yes   Public telephone: No
Walks: Use the adjoining bayfront paved parkways.

Mission Bay   North Cove Park

Description: Small well shaded park with adjacent beach.
Located on Vacation Island off the entry drive, San Diego
Transit service: SDT #9   Schedules: 233-3004
Thomas Guide: Page 52, Grid B/6   On-site parking
Open: 24 Hours   Jurisdiction: City of San Diego   236-6661
Restrooms: Yes   Picnic tables: Yes   Public telephone: No
Walks: There are attractive bayfront paved parkways.

Mission Bay   South Cove Park

Description: Large bayfront grassed park with shade trees.
Located on Vacation Island off the entry drive, San Diego
Transit service: SDT #9   Schedules: 233-3004
Thomas Guide: Page 59, Grid B/1   On-site parking
Open: 24 Hours   Jurisdiction: City of San Diego   236-6661
Restrooms: Yes   Picnic tables: Yes   Public telephone: No
Walks: There are many paved parkways and bayfront paths.

Mission Bay   Sunset Point

Description: Beautiful bayfront park with multiple shade trees.
Located at the West end of Dana Landing Road, San Diego
Transit service: SDT #81   Schedules: 233-3004
Thomas Guide: Page 59, Grid B/2   On-site parking
Open: 24 Hours   Jurisdiction: City of San Diego   236-6661
Restrooms: Yes   Picnic tables: Yes   Public telephone: No
Walks: There are inviting parkways and benches.

Mission Bay   Vacation Island

Description: Private hotel grounds surrounded by public parks.
Located at 1400 West Vacation Road, San Diego
Transit service: SDT #9   Schedules: 233-3004
Thomas Guide: Page 52, Grid B/6 and Page 59, Grid A/1
Open: 24 Hours   Jurisdiction: Princess Hotels, Inc.
Information: 274-4630   Restrooms: Yes   Picnic area: No
Public telephone: Yes   Walks: Private, not for public use.

Mission Bay   Visitor Information Center

Description: Tourist information center with adjoining parks.
Located at 2688 Mission Bay Drive at Clairemont Dr., San Diego
Transit service: SDT #30, #50/150   Schedules: 233-3004
Thomas Guide: Page 52, Grid E/2   On-site parking
Open: 0900 to 1800   Jurisdiction: City of San Diego   236-6661
Restrooms: Yes   Picnic area: Yes   Public telephone: Yes
Walks: There are some parkways and nearby water-front paths.

Mission Beach   Santa Clara Recreation Center

Description: Recreation center, bay front park, tennis, ballfield.
Located at 1008 Santa Clara Place, San Diego
Transit service: SDT #34, #81   Schedules: 233-3004
Thomas Guide: Page 52, Grid B/5   On-site parking
Open: 24 Hours   Jurisdiction: City of San Diego   236-6661
Restrooms: Yes   Picnic tables: Yes   Public telephone: No
Walks: The paved bay-front parkways are recommended.

Mission Hills   Calvary Pioneer Memorial Park

Description: Historical monument/park over an old cemetery.
Located at 1521 Washington Place, San Diego
Transit service: SDT #3, #43   Schedules: 233-3004
Thomas Guide: Page 60, Grid B/3   Street parking
Open: 24 Hours   Jurisdiction: City of San Diego   236-6661
Restrooms: Yes   Picnic tables: Yes   Public telephone: No
Walks: Adjoins Mission Hills parkways and residential area.

Mission Hills

Mission Hills Park

Description: Neighborhood park, tennis, shade trees and totlot.
Located at 1521 Washington Place, San Diego
Transit service: SDT #3, #43   Schedules: 233-3004
Thomas Guide: Page 60, Grid B/3   Street parking
Open: 24 Hours   Jurisdiction: City of San Diego   236-6661
Restrooms: Yes   Picnic tables: Yes   Public telephone: No
Walks: Paved parkway, residential area, adjacent rustic canyon.

Mission Valley

Mission Heights Park

Description: Quiet hilltop parksite with playground, ball court.
Located at 1716 Westinghouse Street, San Diego
Transit service: SDT #25   Schedules: 233-3004
Thomas Guide: Page 53, Grid C/6   Parking at end of Acari St.
Open: 24 Hours   Jurisdiction: City of San Diego   236-6661
Restrooms: No   Picnic area: Yes   Public telephone: No
Walks: Very nice paved parkways and hillside area sidewalks.

Mission Village

Cabrillo Heights Park

Description: Simple 14-acre site; ball fields, soccer and totlot.
Located at 8308 Hurlbut Street, San Diego
Transit service: SDT #16, #25   Schedules: 233-3004
Thomas Guide: Page 53, Grid D/3   Street parking
Open: 24 Hours   Jurisdiction: City of San Diego   236-5710
Restrooms: Yes   Picnic tables/BBQs   Public Telephone: No
Walks: Try a paved parkway in the park and the nearby area.

Moreno

Louis A. Stelzer County Park

Description: Equipped for the handicapped, playground, totlot.
Located on Wildcat Canyon Road, Lakeside
Transit service: No
Thomas Guide: Page 49, Grid B/1   On-site parking
Open: 0930 to 1700 Jurisdiction: County of San Diego 694-3049
Restrooms: Yes   Picnic tables/BBQs   Public telephone: Yes
Walks: Parksite pathways and natural trails in nearby hills.

Morena Village   Lake Morena County Park

Description: Fishing, camping, playground in 3250 acre park.
Located at 2550 Lake Morena Drive, Campo
Transit service: CTS #888, #894   Schedules: 233-3004
Thomas Guide: Page 408, Grid F/4   On-site parking
Open: Dawn to dusk   Jurisdiction: County of S D   694-3049
Restrooms: Yes   Picnic area: Yes   Public telephone: No
Walks: Numerous park trails are maintained for public use.

Mount Helix   Eucalyptus County Park

Description: Rustic eight acre site with playground and totlot.
Located on Bancroft Drive at Mariposa Street, La Mesa
Transit service: No
Thomas Guide: Page 62, Grid E/2   On-site parking
Open: 0600 to 2200   Jurisdiction: County of S D   694-3049
Restrooms: Yes   Picnic tables/BBQs   Public telephone: No
Walks: There are no parkways, adjoining streets are congested.

Mount Helix   Mount Helix County Park

Description: Ten-acre mountain top, superb all-direction view.
Located at the upper end of Mount Helix Drive, La Mesa.
Transit service: No
Thomas Guide: Page 63, Grid A/1   Limited on-site parking.
Open: 0930 to 1900   Jurisdiction: County of S D   694-3049
Restrooms: No   Picnic area: No   Public telephone: No
Walks: Modest size of developed area limits walking potential.

National City   El Toyon Park

Description: Recreation center, ball fields and totlot.
Located at "U" Avenue and First Street, National City
Transit service: NCT #601   Schedules: 233-3004
Thomas Guide: Page 66, Grid C/4   On-site parking
Open: 0800 to 2100 Jurisdiction: City of National City 336-4290
Restrooms: Yes   Picnic tables: Yes   Public telephone: No
Walks: A large site with an excellent grid of paved parkways.

National City **Kimball Park**

Description: Major facility, playing fields, ball courts and totlot.
Located at 12th and "D" Streets, National City
Transit service: NCT #601, #602, #604   Schedules: 233-3004
Thomas Guide: Page 66, Grid B/6   On-site parking
Open: 0800 to 2100   Jurisdiction: City of National City 336-4297
Restrooms: Yes   Picnic tables/BBQs   Public telephone: No
Walks: Many paved and natural parkways for exercise walkers.

National City **Las Palmas Park**

Description: Golf, pool, recreation center, play fields and totlot.
Located at 1800 East 20th Street, National City
Transit service: NCT #602   Schedules: 233-3004
Thomas Guide: Page 66, Grid D/6   On-site parking
Open: 0800 to 2100   Jurisdiction: City of National City   336-4290
Restrooms: Yes   Picnic tables: Yes   Public telephone: No
Walks: Good paved parkways and grassed fields in the park.

Nestor **Berry Park**

Description: Small neighborhood park, shade trees, near school.
Located at 2060 Leon Avenue, San Diego
Transit service: MTS #933, #934   Schedules: 233-3004
Thomas Guide: Page 71. Grid D/6   Street parking
Open: 24 Hours   Jurisdiction: City of San Diego   236-6661
Restrooms: No   Picnic tables: Yes   Public telephone: No
Walks: In the park only, as there are no area sidewalks.

Nestor

South Bay Park

Description: Multipurpose park, gym, play fields and totlot.
Located at 1885 Coronado Avenue, San Diego
Transit service: MTS #933, #934   Schedules: 233-3004
Thomas Guide: Page 71, Grid C/5   On-site parking
Open: 24 Hours   Jurisdiction: City of San Diego   423-3321
Restrooms: Yes   Picnic tables/BBQs   Public telephone: Near
Walks: There are paved parkways and a walkable nearby area.

North City West

Carmel Del Mar Park

Description: Large community park, youth club, fields, totlot.
Located at 4400 Carmel Park Drive, San Diego
Transit service: No
Thomas Guide: Page 34, Grid D/5   On-site parking
Open: 24 Hours   Jurisdiction: City of San Diego   236-6661
Restrooms: Yes   Picnic tables: Yes   Public telephone: Yes
Walks: Excellent in adjoining housing area and paved parkways.

North City West   **Sorrento Highland Park**

Description: Neighborhood park with a totlot, near a school.
Located at 14000 High Bluff Drive, San Diego
Transit service: No
Thomas Guide: Page 34, Grid C/3   Parking off Longwood Drive
Open: 24 Hours   Jurisdiction: City of San Diego   236-6661
Restrooms: No   Picnic tables/BBQs Public telephone: No
Walks: Several parkways and the pleasant nearby area.

North Park   **North Park Recreation Center**

Description: Rec center, tennis, playground, ballfields and totlot.
Located at 4044 Idaho Street, San Diego
Transit service: SDT #1, #6, #7, #15, #115   Schedules: 233-3004
Thomas Guide: Page 60, Grid E/3   Street parking
Open: 24 Hours   Jurisdiction: City of San Diego   565-6515
Restrooms: Yes   Picnic tables/BBQs   Public telephone: No
Walks: There is one parkway and the nearby housing area.

Oak Park   **Chollas Lake Community Park**

Description: Lake, PAR course, playground, ball courts, totlot.
Located at 6350 College Grove Drive, San Diego
Transit service: SDT #5, #16, #36   Schedules: 233-3004
Thomas Guide: Page 61, Grid F/5   On-site parking
Open: 0700 to dusk   Jurisdiction: City of San Diego   265-9855
Restrooms: Yes   Picnic tables/BBQs   Public telephone: Yes
Walks: There is a marked and measured .8-mile loop parkway.

Oak Park   Oak Park Neighborhood Park

Description: Neighborhood park, baseball, some shade, totlot.
Located at 5235 Maple Street, San Diego
Transit service: SDT #5/105   Schedules: 233-3004
Thomas Guide: Page 61, Grid D/5   On-site parking
Open: 24 Hours   Jurisdiction: City of San Diego   236-6661
Restrooms: No   Picnic tables: Yes   Public telephone: No
Walks: Use the parkway and nearby residential area.

Ocean Beach   Collier Community Park

Description: Rec building, gym, ball fields, horseshoes and totlot.
Located at 2312 Famosa Boulevard, San Diego
Transit service: SDT #35   Schedules: 233-3004
Thomas Guide: Page 59, Grid C/3-4   On-site parking
Open: Dawn to dusk   Jurisdiction: City of San Diego   236-5710
Restrooms: Yes   Picnic tables/BBQs   Public telephone: No
Walks: There are excellent long paved parkways.

Ocean Beach   Collier Neighborhood Park West

Description: Pleasant park with shade trees and playground.
Located at 2351 Soto Street, San Diego
Transit service: No
Thomas Guide: Page 59, Grid C/4   Street parking
Open: 24 Hours   Jurisdiction: City of San Diego   236-6661
Restrooms: No   Picnic tables: Yes   Public telephone: No
Walks: Nice grassed parkland or walk in the residential area.

Ocean Beach   **Collier Sunset Park**

Description: A huge grassed playing field.
Located on Sunset Cliffs Road (No. of W.Point Loma), San Diego
Transit service: SDT #34   Schedules: 233-3004
Thomas Guide: Page 59, Grid C/3   On-site parking
Open: 24 Hours   Jurisdiction: City of San Diego   236-6661
Restrooms: Yes   Picnic tables/BBQs   Public telephone: No
Walks: Parkland is available when playing fields not in use.

Ocean Beach   **Mission Bay Park South**

Description: A portion of 4600-acre Mission Bay Parks complex.
Located at 2525 Bacon Street, San Diego
Transit service: SDT #35   Schedules: 233-3004
Thomas Guide: Page 59, Grid B/3   On-site parking
Open: 24 Hours   Jurisdiction: City of San Diego   236-6661
Restrooms: No   Picnic area: No   Public telephone: No
Walks: Parkland and pathway along San Diego River channel.

Ocean Beach   **Ocean Beach Athletic Area (Robb Field)**

Description: Baseball, playing fields, ball courts, tennis, totlot.
Located at 2525 Bacon Street, San Diego
Transit service: SDT #35   Schedules: 233-3004
Thomas Guide: Page 59, Grid B/3   On-site parking
Open: 24 Hours   Jurisdiction: City of San Diego   531-1563
Restrooms: Yes   Picnic tables: Yes   Public telephone: No
Walks: There are paved and natural parkways everywhere.

Ocean Beach

Ocean Beach Community Center

Description: Mini-Park, ball court, shuffleboard and totlot.
Located at 4726 Santa Monica Avenue, San Diego
Transit service: SDT #35 Schedules: 233-3004
Thomas Guide: Page 59, Grid B/4 Street parking
Open: 24 Hours Jurisdiction: City of San Diego 531-1527
Restrooms: Yes Picnic tables: Yes Public telephone: No
Walks: Park is not suitable but the residential area is.

Oceanside

Buddy Todd Memorial Park

Description: Very nice 19 acres of landscaped slopes adjoining
the San Luis Rey River. Ball fields, tot lot and playground.
Located in the 2900 block on Mesa Drive, Oceanside
Transit service: NCTD # 313 Schedules: 722- or 743-6283
Thomas Guide: Page 9, Grid F/5 On-site parking
Open: 0600 to 2100 Jurisdiction: City of Oceanside 966-4530
Restrooms: Yes Picnic tables/BBQs Public telephone: Yes
Walking: Site has random natural paths for a variety of walks.

Oceanside

Capistrano Park

Description: Baseball, playground, ball court, tennis and totlot.
Located at 770 Capistrano Drive, Oceanside
Transit service: NCTD # 316 Schedules: 722- or 743-6283
Thomas Guide: Page 9, Grid C-4 On-site parking
Open: 0600 to 2100 Jurisdiction: City of Oceanside 966-4530
Restrooms: Yes Picnic tables/BBQs Public telephone: Yes
Walks: No sidewalks near park. Several random hillside trails.

Oceanside

Carrasco Park Site

Description: Formerly Skylark Park, presently undeveloped.
Located at Skylark Drive and Downs Street, Oceanside
Transit service: NCTD #316, #318   Schedules: 722 or 743-6283
Thomas Guide: Page 9, Grid E/6   Street parking
Open: Closed   Jurisdiction: City of Oceanside   966-4530
Restrooms: No   Picnic tables: Yes   Public telephone: No
Walks: Neither park site or surrounding streets would be useful.

Oceanside

Fire Mountain Park

Description: Fenced land around a water tank. Locked gate.
Located at 2430 Fire Mountain Road, Oceanside
Transit service: No
Thomas Guide: Page 9, Grid F/6
Open: Closed   Jurisdiction: City of Oceanside   966-4530
Restrooms: No   Picnic area: No   Public Telephone: No
Walks: Property is not open to the public.

Oceanside

Foss Lake

Description: Small lake surrounded by municipal golf course
Located at 825 Douglas Drive, Oceanside
Transit service: NCTD # 303, #309, #313   Info: 722 or 743-6283
Thomas Guide: Page 7, Grid B/2   Golf course parking lot
Open: 0600 to dusk   Jurisdiction: City of Oceanside   966-4530
Restrooms: Yes   Picnic area: No   Public telephone: Yes
Walks: Not feasible due to surrounding golf course activity.

Oceanside

Guajome Regional Park

Description: A 570-acre park with lake fishing, campsites, hiking trails, horseshoe pits, nature center and playgrounds.
Located on Patiences Place, Oceanside
Transit service: NCTD # 306   Schedules: 722- or 743-6283
Thomas Guide: Page 7, Grid F/6   On-site parking, fee
Open: 0930 to 1900 Jurisdiction: County of San Diego 694-3049
Restrooms: Yes   Picnic tables/BBQs   Public telephone: No
Walking: A wide variety of hiking and walking trails are posted.

Oceanside

John H. Landes Park

Description: Area park, rec center, play fields, tennis and totlot.
Located at 2855 Cedar Road, Oceanside
Transit service: NCTD #302   Schedules: 722 or 743-6283
Thomas Guide: Page 10, Grid E/6   On-site parking
Open: Dawn to 2100   Jurisdiction: City of Oceanside   724-2666
Restrooms: Yes   Picnic tables/BBQs   Public telephone: Yes
Walks: Use nearby area sidewalks. Playing fields not suitable.

Oceanside

Libby Lake Park

Description: Nice 14-acre park and lake with playground.
Located at 424 Calle Montecito, Oceanside
Transit service: NCTD #306, #309, #313   Info: 722 or 743-6283
Thomas Guide: Page 7, Grid C/5   Street parking
Open: 0600 to 2100   Jurisdiction: City of Oceanside   966-4530
Restrooms: Yes   Picnic tables/BBQs   Public telephone: No
Walking: Pathway around the lake and random hillside trails.

Park Walking in San Diego County

Oceanside

North River Road Park

Description: Community center, baseball, playgrounds, totlot, tennis and ball courts on a river-front 16-acre site.
Located at 5306 North River Road, Oceanside
Transit service: NCTD #306, #309, #313   Info: 722- or 743-6283
Thomas Guide: Page 7, Grid E/5   On-site parking
Open: 0600 to 2100   Jurisdiction: City of Oceanside   439-5877
Restrooms: Yes   Picnic tables/BBQs   Public telephone: Yes
Walking: Nearby area and a long, flat-top, roadside berm.

Oceanside

Oak Riparian Park

Description: Small children's playground. Some hillside paths.
Located at 4625 Lake Boulevard, Oceanside
Transit service: NCTD #311   Schedules: 722-6283 or 743-6283
Thomas Guide: Page 15, Grid A/2.   Limited on-site parking
Open: 0600 to 2100   Jurisdiction: City of Oceanside   966-4530
Restrooms: Yes   Picnic tables/BBQs   Public telephone: No.
Walking: Adjoining area sidewalks or the hillside trails.

Oceanside

Recreation Park

Description: Twelve-acre center-city park and ballfield complex.
Located in the 300 block on Brooks Street, Oceanside
Transit service: NCTD # 312   Schedules: 722- or 743-6283
Thomas Guide: Page 9, Grid D/5   On-site parking
Open: 0600 to 2100   Jurisdiction: City of Oceanside   966-4530
Restrooms: Yes   Picnic tables/BBQs   Telephone: Nearby
Walks: A residential area on the eastern side is suggested.

Oceanside

Sherbourne Park

Description: Ball fields, ball courts, playground and totlot.
Located midway on Sherbourne Drive, Oceanside
Transit service: NCTD # 311   Schedules: 722- or 743-6283
Thomas Guide: Page 10, Grid D/6   Street parking
Open: 0600 to 2100   Jurisdiction: City of Oceanside   966-4530
Restrooms: Yes   Picnic tables/BBQs   Public telephone: No
Walks: The adjoining residential area is recommended.

Oceanside

South Oceanside Park

Description: Baseball, tennis, playground; adjoining a school.
Located at Stewart Street and Cassidy Street, Oceanside
Transit service: NCTD #312   Schedules: 722 or 743-6283
Thomas Guide: Page 13, Grid E/2   Street parking
Open: 0900 to 2100   Jurisdiction: City of Oceanside   966-4530
Restrooms: No   Picnic area: No   Public telephone: No
Walks: Would be better in the nearby residential area.

Old Town

Heritage Park

Description: Restored Victorian homes on eight-acre park site.
Located on Heritage Park Row, San Diego
Transit service: SDT #4, #5/105, #6   Schedules: 233-3004
Thomas Guide: Page 59, Grid F/3   Parking adjacent
Open: 24 Hours   Jurisdiction: County of San Diego   694-3049
Restrooms: Yes   Picnic area: No   Public telephone: No
Walks: Well worth a visit for sightseeing and strolling.

Old Town   Old Town State Historical Park

Description: 13-Acre restoration of historical San Diego City.
Located at 4002 Wallace Street, San Diego
Transit service: SDT #4, #5/105, #6   Schedules: 233-3004
Thomas Guide: Page 59, Grid F/3   On-site parking
Open: 24 Hours   Jurisdiction: State of California   237-6770
Restrooms: Yes   Picnic area: Yes   Public telephone: Yes
Walks: Adjoins Heritage Park for sightseeing and strolling.

Old Town   Presidio Park

Description: Serra Mission Church, city overview, shade trees.
Located at 3339 Taylor Street, San Diego
Transit service: SDT #4, #5/105, #6, #105   Schedules: 233-3004
Thomas Guide: Page 59, Grid F/2   On-site parking
Open: 24 Hours   Jurisdiction: City of San Diego   297-8359
Restrooms: Yes   Picnic tables: Yes   Public telephone: Yes
Walks: Hillsides are not suitable. Several parkways are.

Olivenhain   **Shea Homes Recreation Trails**

Description: Equestrian/hiking trails in a housing development.
Located on Bumann Road, off Fortuna Ranch Road, Encinitas
Transit service: No
Thomas Guide: Page 25, Grid F/3   Street parking
Open: Dawn to dusk   Jurisdiction: City of Encinitas   944-5050
Restrooms: No   Picnic area: No   Public telephone: No
Walks: Suitable for hiking. Not maintained as walking paths.

Otay   **Loma Verde Park**

Description: About six-acres of grassed parkland with gazebo,
pool, playground, recreation center and totlot. Joins S.D.G.& E.
Located at 1420 Loma Lane, Chula Vista
Transit service: CVT #701   Schedules: 233-3004
Thomas Guide: Page 72, Grid A/2   Street parking
Open: 0700 to 2230   Jurisdiction: City of Chula Vista   691-5071
Restrooms: Yes   Picnic tables: Yes   Public telephone: No
Walks: Excellent on the grass field and wandering parkways.

Otay   **Orange Avenue Fields**

Description: A primary baseball facility for the community.
Located at 160 Orange Avenue, Chula Vista
Transit service: CVT #702/702A   Schedules: 233-3004
Thomas Guide: Page 71, Grid E/2   On-site parking
Open: 0700 to 2230   Jurisdiction: City of Chula Vista   691-5071
Restrooms: Yes   Picnic area: No   Public telephone: No
Walks: Parksite could be used when baseball fields are not in us.

Otay   Otay Park

Description: Neighborhood five-acre park, playfield and totlot.
Located at 1613 Albany Avenue, Chula Vista
Transit service: SDT #29   Schedules: 233-3004
Thomas Guide: Page 71, Grid F/2   Street parking
Open: 0700 to 2230   Jurisdiction: City of Chula Vista   691-5071
Restrooms: Yes   Picnic tables/BBQs   Public telephone: No
Walks: The few parkways and nearby area are walkable.

Otay   Palomar Park

Description: Quiet neighborhood park, playground, totlot, shade.
Located at 1350 Palomar Drive, Chula Vista
Transit service: CVT #702, #703   Schedules: 233-3004
Thomas Guide: Page 72, Grid B/1   Limited street parking
Open: 0700 to 2230   Jurisdiction: City of Chula Vista   691-5071
Restrooms: No   Picnic tables/BBQs   Public telephone: No
Walk: Nice parkways and surrounding area for walks.

Otay   SDG&E Park East-West

Description: 20-Acres adjoining Loma Verde Park's play area.
Located at 1450 Hilltop Drive, Chula Vista
Transit service: CVT #701   Schedules: 233-3004
Thomas Guide: Page 72, Grid A/2   Limited on-site parking
Open: 0700 to 2230   Jurisdiction: City of Chula Vista   691-5071
Restrooms: No   Picnic tables/shade   Public Telephone: No
Walks: An excellent site for long meadow walks

Otay   Valle Lindo Park

Description: Four-acres with playground, fields and ball courts.
Located at 545 Sequoia Street, Chula Vista
Transit service: CVT #703   Schedules: 233-3004
Thomas Guide: Page 72, Grid C/2   Street parking
Open: 0700 to 2230   Jurisdiction: City of Chula Vista   691-5071
Restrooms: No   Picnic area: Yes   Public telephone: No
Walks: Parksite and adjoining areas are very walkable.

Otay Mesa   Howard Lane Park

Description: Neighborhood park, ball court, tennis and totlot.
Located at Dairy Mart Road and Beyer Boulevard, San Diego
Transit service: SDT #29, #932, S D Trolley   Schedule: 233-3004
Thomas Guide: Page 71, Grid F/6   Street parking
Open: 24 Hours   Jurisdiction: City of San Diego   236-6661
Restrooms: Yes   Picnic tables/BBQs   Public telephone: No
Walks: A few short parkways but the nearby area is better.

Otay Mesa   Montgomery-Waller Park

Description: Rec center; playing fields, tennis, ballcourts, totlot
Located at 3060 Palm Avenue, San Diego
Transit service: SDT #33/33A   Schedules: 233-3004
Thomas Guide: Page 71, Grid E/4   On-site parking
Open: 24 Hours   Jurisdiction: City of San Diego   236-6661
Restrooms: Yes   Picnic tables: Yes   Public telephone: No
Walks: Many fine parkways plus a nice residential area.

Otay Mesa   Palm Ridge Park

Description: Large playground, ballfields, ballcourts and totlot.
Located at 751 Firethorn Street, San Diego
Transit service: No
Thomas Guide: Page 72, Grid B/4   On-site parking
Open: 24 Hours   Jurisdiction: City of San Diego   236-6661
Restrooms: Yes   Picnic area: No   Public telephone: No
Walks: An excellent loop parkway and in the nearby area.

Otay Mesa   Silver Wing Park

Description: Playing fields, ball court, totlot and rec center.
Located at 3737 Arey Drive, San Diego
Transit service: SDT #29, MTS #933/934   Schedules: 233-3004
Thomas Guide: Page 72, Grid A/5   On-site parking
Open: 24 Hours   Jurisdiction: City of San Diego   424-7845
Restrooms: Yes   Picnic tables: Yes   Public telephone: No
Walks: Many paved parkways and the nearby residential area.

Otay Mesa   **Vista Terrace Park**

Description: San Ysidro Public Pool, playing fields and totlot.
Located at 301 Athey Avenue, San Diego
Transit service: MTS #932   Schedules: 233-3004
Thomas Guide: Page 72, Grid A/6   On-site parking
Open: 24 Hours (Park) Jurisdiction: City of San Diego 236-6661
Restrooms: Yes   Picnic area: No   Public telephone: No
Walks: Park site is not suitable and the area not recommended.

Pacific Beach   **Kate O. Sessions Park**

Description: A fine major park with all facilities and a totlot.
Located at 5115 Soledad Road, San Diego
Transit service: No
Thomas Guide: Page 52, Grid C/2   On-site parking
Open: 24 Hours   Jurisdiction: City of San Diego   236-6661
Restrooms: Yes   Picnic tables: Yes   Public telephone: No
Walks: Several paved parkways and 80 acres of grassed slopes.

Pacific Beach   **Pacific Beach Recreation Center**

Description: Recreation building with ball court and totlot.
Located at 1405 Diamond Street, San Diego
Transit service: SDT #9, #27   Schedules: 233-3004
Thomas Guide: Page 52, Grid B/4   Street parking
Open: 24 Hours   Jurisdiction: City of San Diego   490-0927
Restrooms: Yes   Picnic area: No   Public telephone: No
Walks: Park is not suitable. Use adjoining residential area.

Pala   **Wilderness Gardens County Park**

Description: Trails, ponds and play areas on a 585-acre site.
Located nine miles east of I-l5 on Hiway 76, past Pala.
Transit service: No
Thomas Guide: Page 400, Grid D/3   On-site parking fee
Open: 0930-1700   Jurisdiction: County of San Diego   694-3049
Restrooms: Yes   Picnic tables/fire rings Public telephone: No
Walking: An under-rated County Park, superb marked trails.

Palomar Mountain
Palomar Mountain County Park

Description: Two-acre picnic site in mountain hiking area.
Located on Birch Hill Rd off Crestline Rd, Palomar Mountain
Transit service: No
Thomas Guide: Page 401, Grid A/3　　　　On-site parking
Open: 0930 to 1900　Jurisdiction: County of S D　694-3049
Restrooms: Yes　　　Picnic tables/BBQs　Public telephone: No
Walks: There are a few random hiking trails in the vicinity.

Palomar Mountain
Palomar Mountain State Park

Description: Camping and hiking in 1900-acre mountain park.
Located at 19552 State Park Road, Palomar Mountain
Transit service: No
Thomas Guide: Page 400, Grid F/3　　　　On-site parking fee
Open: Dawn to dusk　Jurisdiction: State of California　742-3462
Restrooms: Yes　　　Picnic tables/BBQs　Public telephone: Yes
Walks: At entry gate request map for location of the many trails.

Palo Verde
Palo Verde Lake

Description: Private lake and recreation area near Alpine.
Located at 4090 Via Palo Verde Lago, Alpine
Transit service: No
Thomas Guide: Page 58-R, Grid E/2
Open: Closed to public use　　　Jurisdiction: Palo Verde Ranch
Information: 445-9250　　　Restrooms: No　　Picnic area: No
Telephone: No　　　　　　Walks: Not open for public use.

Paradise Hills
Bay Terrace Community Park

Description: Neighborhood park, play fields, playground, totlot.
Located at 7373 Toomas Street, San Diego
Transit service: SDT DART　　　　　Schedules: 293-3278
Thomas Guide: Page 67, Grid B/5　　　　On-site parking
Open: 0600 to 2200　Jurisdiction: City of San Diego　236-6661
Restrooms: Yes　　　Picnic tables: Yes　　Public telephone: No
Walks: Paved parkways and the residential area are useful.

Paradise Hills   **Lomita Park**

Description: Neighborhood play field, ball court and playground.
Located at 8205 Leucadia Avenue, San Diego
Transit service: SDT #4   Schedules: 233-3004
Thomas Guide: Page 67, Grid C/2   Street parking
Open: 24 Hours   Jurisdiction: City of San Diego   236-6661
Restrooms: No   Picnic tables: Yes   Public telephone: No
Walks: Lacks shade and lengthy parkways.

Paradise Hills   **Martin Luther King Jr. Park**

Description: An impressive recreation facility with gymnasium,
tennis, ball courts, pool, play fields and totlot.
Located at 6401 Skyline Drive, San Diego
Transit service: SDT #11   Schedules: 233-3004
Thomas Guide: Page 66, Grid F/3   On-site parking
Open: 24 Hours   Jurisdiction: City of San Diego   262-4063
Restrooms: Yes   Picnic tables: Yes   Public telephone: No
Walks: Paved parkways and in the nearby residential area.

Paradise Hills   **Paradise Hills Community Park**

Description: Recreation center, playground, ballfields and totlot.
Located at 6610 Potomac Street, San Diego
Transit service: SDT DART   Schedules: 293-3278
Thomas Guide: Page 67, Grid A/4   On-site parking
Open: 24 Hours   Jurisdiction: City of San Diego   475-0632
Restrooms: Yes   Picnic tables: Yes   Public telephone: No
Walks: There are many paved and natural parkways.

Paradise Hills   Penn Athletic Field

Description: Large baseball complex, rec. room and small totlot.
Located at 2250 Dusk Drive, San Diego
Transit service: SDT DART   Schedules: 293-3278
Thomas Guide: Page 67, Grid A/5   Limited on-site parking
Open:; 24 Hours   Jurisdiction: City of San Diego   470-4547
Restrooms: Yes   Picnic tables: Yes   Public telephone: No
Walks: Not when ballfields in use. Residential area is suitable.

Paradise Hills   Skyline Park

Description: Gymnasium, baseball fields, ball courts and totlot.
Located at 8285 Skyline Drive, San Diego
Transit service: SDT #4, #11   Schedules: 233-3004
Thomas Guide: Page 67, Grid C/2   Limited on-site parking
Open: 24 Hours   Jurisdiction: City of San Diego   479-7712
Restrooms: Yes   Picnic tables: Yes   Public telephone: No
Walks: Paved parkways are best due to heavy traffic in area.

Paradise Hills   Skyview Park

Description: Neighborhood playground, PAR course and totlot.
Located at 7250 Skyline Drive, San Diego
Transit service: SDT #11   Schedules: 233-3004
Thomas Guide: Page 67, Grid B/2   Street parking
Open: 24 Hours   Jurisdiction: City of San Diego   236-6661
Restrooms: No   Picnic tables: Yes   Public telephone: Yes
Walks: Possible on the paved parkway and in the nearby area.

Pine Valley   Pine Valley County Park

Description: Rural park, tennis, ballfield, playground and totlot.
Located at 28800 Pine Valley Road, Pine Valley
Transit service: CTS #888   Schedules: 233-3004
Thomas Guide: Page 51-W, Grid C/4   On-site parking fee
Open: 0930 to 1700 Jurisdiction: County of San Diego 694-3049
Restrooms: Yes Picnic tables/BBQs Public telephone: Nearby
Walks: 17 Acres with parksite trails and adjoining rural roads.

Point Loma   **Cabrillo National Monument**

Description: Unique national park overlooks San Diego Harbor.
Located at the end of Cabrillo Memorial Drive, Point Loma
Transit service: SDT #6   Schedules: 233-3004
Thomas Guide: Page 64, Grid B/6   On-site parking fee
Open: 0900 to 1715   Jurisdiction: Dept. of Interior   557-5450
Restrooms: Yes   Picnic area: Yes   Public telephone: Yes
Walks: The posted "Bayside Trail" is open daily.

Potrero   **Mason Wildlife County Park**

Description: A nature preserve not presently open for visits.
Located off Harris Ranch Road, Potrero
Transit service: CTS #846, #847   Schedules: 233-3004
Thomas Guide: Page 408, Grid E/5   Street parking
Open: Closed   Jurisdiction: County of San Diego   694-3049
Restrooms: No   Picnic area: No   Public telephone: No
Walks: The nature preserve has no means of public access.

Potrero   **Potrero County Park**

Description: Camping, play and ball fields, totlot, horseshoes.
Located at the end of Potrero Park Drive, Potrero
Transit service: CTS #894   Schedules: 233-3004
Thomas Guide: Page 408, Grid E/5   On-site parking fee
Open: 0930 to 1800 Jurisdiction: County of San Diego 694-3049
Restrooms: Yes   Picnic tables/BBQs   Public telephone: Yes
Walks: Excellent parksite hiking plus a self-guided nature trail.

Poway

Blue Sky Ecological Preserve

Description: A hiker's park in the early stages of development.
Located at 16400 Espola Road, Poway
Transit service: CTS #844, #845   Schedules: 233-3004
Thomas Guide: Page 33, Grid D/2   Street parking
Open: 24 Hours   Jurisdiction: City of Poway   695-1400
Restrooms: No   Picnic area: No   Public telephone: No
Walks: Presently (1991) best for experienced hikers only.

Poway

Lake Poway Park

Description: A superb recreation facility with lake-front fields,
boat rentals, hiking trails, campsites, playground and totlot.
Located at 14644 Lake Poway Road, Poway
Transit service: CTS #844, #845   Schedules: 233-3004
Thomas Guide: Page 33. Grid E/3   On-site parking fee
Open: Dawn to dusk   Jurisdiction: City of Poway   748-2224
Restrooms: Yes   Picnic tables/BBQs   Public telephone: Yes
Walking: Random lakefront and hillside trails. Maps available.

Park Walking in San Diego County

Poway   Poway Community Park

Description: Center-city auditorium, tennis, baseball and totlot.
Located at 13094 Bowron Road, Poway
Transit service: CTS 843, #844, #845   Schedules: 233-3004
Thomas Guide: Page 37, Grid B/4   Plentiful on-site parking
Open: Dawn to dusk   Jurisdiction: City of Poway   748-1892
Restrooms: Yes   Picnic tables: Yes   Public telephone: Yes
Walks: On several parkways and the adjoining residential area.

Poway   Starridge Park

Description: Medium-size neighborhood park, play fields, totlot.
Located at 137 Starridge Street, Poway
Transit service: CTS #843, #844, #845   Schedules: 233-3004
Thomas Guide: Page 37, Grid A/2   Parking off Carriage Rd.
Open: Dawn to dusk   Jurisdiction: City of Poway   695-1400
Restrooms: Yes   Picnic tables/BBQs   Public telephone: No
Walks: In the park, adjoining nature trails and residential area.

Poway   Val Verde Park

Description: Playing field, baseball and totlot on about ten acres.
Located at 14600 Valle Verde Road, Poway
Transit service: CTS #844, #845   Schedules: 233-3004
Thomas Guide: Page 33, Grid B/2   On-site parking
Open: Dawn to dusk   Jurisdiction: City of Poway   695-1400
Restrooms: Yes   Picnic tables/BBQs   Public telephone: No
Walks: Use the parkways and nearby pleasant residential areas.

Ramona   Collier County Park

Description: Eight acres, playground, ball courts, tennis, totlot.
Located at Sixth and "E" Streets, Ramona
Transit service: NCTD #307, FAST   Schedules: 722 or 743-6283
Thomas Guide: Page 28-P, Grid F/6   Limited on-site parking
Open: 0930 to 2000 Jurisdiction: County of San Diego 694-3049
Restrooms: Yes   Picnic tables/BBQs   Public telephone: No
Walks: Paved parkways only. There are no area sidewalks.

Ramona   Ramona Community Park

Description: Ballfields, horse ring, ball courts, rec buildings.
Located at the North-West end of Fifth Street, Ramona
Transit service: CTS #881, #882, #883, #884, #885 Info.233-3004
Thomas Guide: Page 28-P, Grid F/5   On-site parking
Open: 24 Hours   Jurisdiction: Ramona Municipal Water Dist.
Information: 789-1330   Restrooms: Yes   Picnic area: Yes
Public telephone: No   Walks: There are some natural trails but
no paved parkways for walking.

Ramona   Ramona Dam

Description: Isolated rural area with random hiking trails.
Located at the end of Green Valley Truck Trail, Ramona
Transit service: No   (An unpaved road)
Thomas Guide: Page 28-N, Grid A/5   Roadside parking
Open: 24 Hours   Jurisdiction: Ramona Municipal Water Dist.
Information: 789-1300   Restrooms: No   Picnic area: No
Public telephone: No   Walks: For the experienced hiker only.

Rancho Bernardo   Rancho Bernardo Park

Description: Lawn bowling, baseball, totlot, tennis, Sr. Center.
Located at 18405 West Bernardo Drive, San Diego
Transit service: No
Thomas Guide: Page 27, Grid E/5   On-site parking
Open: 24 Hours   Jurisdiction: City of San Diego   484-0725
Restrooms: Yes   Picnic area: Yes   Public telephone: Yes
Walking: There are paved walkways in the park site and wide
open grassed play areas suitable for walking. No sidewalks.

Rancho Penasquitos

Black Mountain Park

Description: A large undeveloped park site with fine viewpoints.
Located on Black Mountain Road at Park Drive, San Diego
Transit service: No   (Graded unpaved road)
Thomas Guide: Page 32, Grid A/5   On-site parking below peak
Open: 0900 to 1700   Jurisdiction: City of San Diego   236-6661
Restrooms: No   Picnic area: No   Public telephone: No
Walks: There are a number of random trails to area viewpoints.

Rancho Penasquitos

Rolling Hills Park

Description: Six acres, handball, playground, ball courts, totlot.
Located at 11082 Carlotta Street, San Diego
Transit service: No
Thomas Guide: Page 32, Grid D/5   Street Parking
Open: 24 Hours   Jurisdiction: City of San Diego   236-6661
Restrooms: No   Picnic tables: Yes   Public telephone: No
Walks: Short paved parkway and in an upscale residential area.

Rancho Penasquitos

Twin Trails Park

Description: Playground, tennis, ballfield and grassed areas.
Located at 8990 Twin Trails Drive, San Diego
Transit service: No
Thomas Guide: Page 35, Grid F/3   Street parking
Open: 24 Hours   Jurisdiction: City of San Diego   236-6661
Restrooms: No   Picnic tables: Yes   Public telephone: No
Walks: Paved parkway and nearby upscale residential area.

Rancho San Diego

Del Parque County Park

Description: An undeveloped park site.
Located at 10470 Via del Parque, Spring Valley
Transit service: No
Thomas Guide: Page 63, Grid B/5   Street parking
Open: 24 Hours   Jurisdiction: County of San Diego   694-3049
Restrooms: No   Picnic area: No   Public telephone: No
Walks: Not open for public use.

Rancho Santa Fe

San Dieguito County Park

Description: Hiking trails, playfields and totlot on 122 acres.
Located at Highland Drive & Sun Valley Road, Rancho Santa Fe
Transit service: No
Thomas Guide: Page 30, Grid C/4   On-site parking fee
Open: 0930 to dusk Jurisdiction: County of San Diego 694-3049
Restrooms: Yes   Picnic tables/BBQs   Public telephone: No
Walks: There are an abundance of marked park trails.
Nature-walk guidance is available from the Ranger.

Rolando

Clay Park

Description: Ballcourt, tennis, playground and grass play fields.
Located at 4767 Seminole Avenue, San Diego
Transit service: SDT #15, #115   Schedules: 233-3004
Thomas Guide: Page 61, Grid F/2   Street parking
Open: 24 Hours   Jurisdiction: City of San Diego   236-6661
Restrooms: No   Picnic tables: Yes   Public telephone: No
Walks: There is a nice paved loop parkway and residential area.

Rolando

Colina del Sol Park

Description: Large; with tennis, ball courts, play field and totlot.
Located at 5319 Orange Avenue, San Diego
Transit service: SDT #7, #15, #105, #115   Schedules: 233-3004
Thomas Guide: Page 61, Grid D/3   On-site parking
Open: 24 Hours   Jurisdiction: City of San Diego   583-0303
Restrooms: Yes   Picnic tables/BBQs   Public telephone: No
Walks: Use the variety of paved parkways and nearby area.

Rolando   **Montezuma Park**

Description: Small neighborhood park with nice shade trees.
Located at 4929 Catoctin Drive, San Diego
Transit service: SDT #15, #81   Schedules: 233-3004
Thomas Guide: Page 61, Grid F/1   Street parking
Open: 24 Hours   Jurisdiction: City of San Diego   236-6661
Restrooms: No   Picnic tables: Yes   Public telephone: No
Walks: Short paved parkway and the adjoining residential area.

Rosemont   **Dos Picos County Park**

Description: Peaceful 78-acre valley; camping, playground,
totlot, horseshoes, lake, 7000-year old indian acorn moteros.
Located at 17901 Dos Picos Road, Ramona
Transit service: No
Thomas Guide: Page 33-N/Grid E/5   On-site parking fee
Open: 0930 to 1900 Jurisdiction: County of San Diego 565-3600
Restrooms: Yes   Picnic tables/BBQs   Public telephone: Yes
Walks: There are many fine park-site hiking trails.

Roseville   **Cabrillo Park North**

Description: A very small Mini-Park behind family housing.
Located at 3232 Trumbull Street, San Diego
Transit service: SDT #29   Schedules: 233-3004
Thomas Guide: Page 59, Grid B/6   Street parking
Open: 24 Hours   Jurisdiction: City of San Diego   236-6661
Restrooms: No   Picnic area: No   Public telephone: No
Walks: In the surrounding residential district only.

Roseville   **Cabrillo Park South**

Description: A very small Mini-Park behind family housing.
Located at 1023 Leroy Street, San Diego
Transit service: SDT #29   Schedules: 233-3004
Thomas Guide: Page 59, Grid C/6   ·   Street parking
Open: 24 Hours   Jurisdiction: City of San Diego   236-6661
Restrooms: No   Picnic area: No   Public telephone: No
Walks: In the surrounding residential district.

Roseville   Cabrillo Recreation Center

Description: A community recreation center with tennis, ball
court and play area; shared with adjacent school.
Located at 3051 Canon Street, San Diego
Transit service: SDT #29   Schedules: 233-3004
Thomas Guide: Page 59, Grid C/6   Street parking
Open: 24 Hours   Jurisdiction: City of San Diego   531-1534
Restrooms: Yes   Picnic area: No   Public telephone: No
Walks: Adjoining residential area best for exercise walking.

Roseville   Point Loma Community Park

Description: Community baseball fields and playground.
Located at 1049 Catalina Boulevard, San Diego
Transit service: SDT #6   Schedules: 233-3004
Thomas Guide: Page 59, Grid B/6   On-site parking
Open: 24 Hours   Jurisdiction: City of San Diego   236-6661
Restrooms: Yes   Picnic area: No   Public telephone: No
Walks: Several short paved parkways and the residential area.

San Carlos   San Carlos Park

Description: A large multi-purpose community area with playing
fields, tennis, recreation building and totlot.
Located at 6445 Lake Badin Avenue, San Diego
Transit service: SDT #115, CTS #854   Schedules: 233-3004
Thomas Guide: Page 55, Grid C/4   On-site parking
Open: 24 Hours   Jurisdiction: City of San Diego   461-6131
Restrooms: Yes   Picnic tables/BBQs   Public telephone: No
Walking: Has both paved and unpaved parkways for walking.

San Diego Country Estates   Mount Gower Preserve

Description: 1574 Primitive acres formerly Swartz Canyon Park.
Located at 17090 Gunn Stage Road, Ramona
Transit service: No
Thomas Guide: Page 33-Q, Grid E/2   Limited on-site parking
Open: 0930 to dusk Jurisdiction: County of San Diego 694-3049
Restrooms: No   Picnic area: No   Public telephone: No
Walks: Five miles of hiking trails with more underway.

San Luis Rey   **Fireside Park**

Description: Four-Acre neighborhood park with a playground.
Located at 300 Fireside Drive, Oceanside
Transit service: NCTD # 313   Schedules: 722- or 743-6283
Thomas Guide: Page 10, Grid A/2   Street parking
Open: 0600 to 2100   Jurisdiction: City of Oceanside   966-4530
Restrooms: No   Picnic tables/BBQs   Public telephone: No
Walks: The adjoining residential area would be best.

San Luis Rey   **Heritage Park**

Description: Lovingly restored historic buildings on park site.
Located at 500 Peyri Drive, Oceanside
Transit service: NCTD # 303, # 309, #313 Info: 722- or 743-6283
Thomas Guide: Page 10, Grid B/2   Limited street parking
Open: 0730 to 1600   Jurisdiction: City of Oceanside   966-4530
Restrooms: Yes   Picnic tables: Yes   Public telephone: No
Walks: Best for a strolling visit. Area streets not walkable.

San Luis Rey   **Ivey Ranch Park**

Description: A special park and playground for the handicapped.
Located at 4101 Mission Avenue, Oceanside
Transit service: NCTD # 313   Schedules: 722- or 743-6283
Thomas Guide: Page 10, Grid C/2   On-site parking
Open: 0600 to 2100   Jurisdiction: City of Oceanside   966-4530
Restrooms: Yes   Picnic tables/BBQs   Public telephone: Yes
Walks: Not feasible in park or on adjoining traffic-heavy streets.

San Marcos   **Helen Bougher Memorial Park**

Description: Delightful small park as a fine base for area walks.
Located at the corner of Borden and Bougher Roads, San Marcos
Transit service: NCTD #341   Schedules: 722 or 743-6283
Thomas Guide: Page 17, Grid A/4   Street parking
Open: Dawn/Dusk   Jurisdiction: City of San Marcos   744-1875
Restrooms: No   Picnic tables: Yes   Public Telephone: No
Walks: Excellent lunch stop after walking the residential area.

San Marcos **San Marcos City Park**

Description: Recreation center, playground and City Museum.
Located at 150 East San Marcos Boulevard, San Marcos
Transit service: NCTD #341   Schedules: 722-6283 or 743-6283
Thomas Guide: Page 16, Grid D/6   On-site parking
Open: Dawn to dusk   Jurisdiction: City of San Marcos 744-1875
Restrooms: Yes   Picnic tables: Yes   Public telephone: Yes
Walking: Street configuration, small size and lack of sidewalks
make this park most useful for picnics and visiting the Museum.

San Marcos **Walnut Grove Park**

Description: Barren park with horse arena and playground.
Located at 2200 Sycamore Drive, San Marcos
Transit service: No
Thomas Guide: Page 16, Grid E/2   On-site parking
Open: 0900 To dusk   Jurisdiction: City of San Marcos   744-1875
Restrooms: Yes   Picnic tables/BBQs   Public telephone: No.
Walking: Neither park nor area streets are suitable for walking.

San Marcos **William R. Bradley Park**

Description: Ballfields, tennis, PAR course, day-care and totlot.
Located at 1535 Linda Vista Drive, San Marcos
Transit service: NCTD #341, #304   Schedules: 722 or 743-6283
Thomas Guide: Page 15, Grid F/6   Limited on-site parking
Open: Dawn to Dusk Jurisdiction: City of San Marcos 744-1875
Restrooms: Yes   Picnic tables: Yes   Public telephone: Yes
Walking: No parkways. Only a few adjacent streets are suitable.

Park Walking in San Diego County

San Marcos
Woodland Park

Description: Pool with waterslide, large children's play area and totlot, on a beautifully maintained sloping park site.
Located at 671 Bougher Road, San Marcos
Transit service: NCTD #341 Schedules: 722-6283 or 743-6283
Thomas Guide: Page 17, Grid A/5 On-site parking
Open: 0700 to 2200 Jurisdiction: City of San Marcos 744-1875
Restrooms: Yes Picnic tables/BBQs Public telephone: No
Walking: Woodland is suitable for walks over grassed fields.

San Onofre
San Mateo Campground/Park

Description: On Camp Pendleton, little shade, caravan use.
Located at 830 Christianitos Road, San Clemente
Transit service: NCTD #305 Schedules: 722 or 743-6283
Thomas Guide: Page 403,Grid A/4 On-site parking
Open: 24-Hours Jurisdiction: State of California 237-7411
Restrooms: Yes Picnic tables/fire pits Public telephone: No
Walks: A two-mile path to ocean beach for coast walking.

San Pasqual
San Pasqual Battlefield State Park

Description: Park on site of battle between Mexico and the U.S.
Located at 15808 San Pasqual Valley Road, Escondido
Transit service: NCTD #307 Schedules: 722 or 743-6283
Thomas Guide: Page 404, Grid E/2 On-site parking
Open: 1000 to 1700 Mon-Thur Jurisdiction: State of California
Information: 283-3380 Restrooms: Yes Picnic area: No
Telephone: No Walks: In small site only; area is not suitable.

Santee
Big Rock Park

Description: Tennis, horseshoes, ballcourt, playground, totlot.
Located at 8125 Arlette Street, Santee
Transit service: CTS #846, #847 Schedules: 233-3004
Thomas Guide: Page 47, Grid D/6 On-site parking
Open: 0700 to 1800/2030 Jurisdiction: City of Santee 562-6153
Restrooms: Yes Picnic tables/BBQs Public telephone: Yes
Walks: There are paved parkways and a nearby residential area.

Santee

Description: A pleasant park, PAR course, playground, totlot.
Located at 9125 Carlton Hills Boulevard, Santee
Transit service: CST #846, #847   Schedules: 233-3004
Thomas Guide: Page 47, Grid E/4   On-site parking
Open: 0700 to 1800/2030   Jurisdiction: City of Santee   562-6153
Restrooms: Yes   Picnic tables/BBQs   Public telephone: Yes
Walks: Fine parkways and the adjoining San Diego River trails.

Santee

Description: A chain of lakes with camping, playgrounds, shade.
Located at 9040 Carlton Oaks Drive, Santee
Transit service: CTS #846, #847   Schedules: 233-3004
Thomas Guide: Page 47, Grid E/3-4   On-site parking
Open: Dawn to dusk   Jurisdiction: Padre Dam Water District
Information: 448-2482   Restrooms: Yes   Picnic areas: Yes
Telephone: Yes   Walks: Numerous trails and paved park lanes.

Santee **Woodglen Vista Park**

Description: Very nice; baseball, tennis, playground and totlot.
Located at 10250 Woodglen Vista Drive, Santee
Transit service: CTS #846, #847   Schedules: 233-3004
Thomas Guide: Page 48 Grid A/2   On-site parking
Open: 0700 to 1800/2030   Jurisdiction: City of Santee   562-6153
Restrooms: Yes   Picnic tables/BBQs   Public telephone: No
Walks: Paved parkways and in the surrounding residential area.

San Ysidro **San Ysidro Athletic Area**

Description: A large complex of baseball and soccer fields.
Located at Camino de la Plaza and Willow Road, San Ysidro
Transit service: MTS #932   Schedules: 233-3004
Thomas Guide: Page 74, Grid B/2   On-site parking
Open: 24 Hours   Jurisdiction: City of San Diego   236-6661
Restrooms: Yes   Picnic tables/BBQs   Public telephone: No
Walks: Only in the park site when fields are not in use.

San Ysidro **San Ysidro Park**

Description: Senior center, tennis, ball courts, turf and totlot.
Located at San Ysidro Boulevard and Park Drive, San Ysidro
Transit service: SD Trolley   Schedules: 233-3004
Thomas Guide: Page 174, Grid B/1   Street parking
Open: 24 Hours   Jurisdiction: City of San Diego   236-6661
Restrooms: Yes   Picnic tables/BBQs   Telephone: Nearby
Walks: Sidewalks are very busy. Park turfed area is walkable.

San Ysidro **San Ysidro Recreation Center**

Description: Senior center with gymnasium and meeting room.
Located at 179 Diza Road, San Ysidro
Transit service: No
Thomas Guide: Page 72, Grid B/6   Street parking
Open: 24 Hours   Jurisdiction: City of San Diego   428-8079
Restrooms: Yes   Picnic area: No   Public telephone: Yes
Walks: No parkways. Surrounding residential area for walking.

San Ysidro

Sunset County Park

Description: Portion of planned Tijuana River Regional Park.
Located on Sunset Avenue near Saturn Boulevard, San Ysidro
Transit service: No
Thomas Guide: Page 73, Grid C/1   Street parking
Open: Closed   Jurisdiction: County of San Diego   694-3049
Restrooms: No   Picnic area: No   Public telephone: No
Walks: Undeveloped open space not suitable for walks.

Scripps Miramar Ranch

Forestview Mini-Park

Description: A mini Mini-Park with playground equipment.
Located at 11210 Forestview Lane, San Diego
Transit service: No
Thomas Guide: Page 40, Grid D/2   Street parking
Open: 24 Hours   Jurisdiction: City of San Diego   236-6661
Restrooms: No   Picnic area: No   Public telephone: No
Walks: Only in the adjoining upscale residential area.

Scripps Miramar Ranch

Jarabek Park

Description: Large park, play fields, tennis, totlot, PAR course.
Located at 10050 Avenida Magnifica, San Diego
Transit service: No
Thomas Guide: Page 40, Grid D/3   On-site parking
Open: 24 Hours   Jurisdiction: City of San Diego   236-6661
Restrooms: Yes   Picnic tables: Yes   Public Telephone: No
Walks: There are a number of parkways and area walk sites.

Scripps Miramar Ranch   **Lake Miramar Reservoir**

Description: A fine facility showcasing a large lake, with hiking trails and fishing (permit required) amid peaceful surroundings.
Located on Scripps Lake Drive, San Diego
Transit service: SDT DART   Schedules: 293-3278
Thomas Guide: Page 40, Grid C/2   On-site parking
Open: Dawn to dusk   Jurisdiction: City of San Diego   465-4500
Restrooms: Yes   Picnic tables/BBQs Public telephone: Yes
Walking: Many random paths and hiking trails around the lake.

Scripps Miramar Ranch   **Semillon Mini-Park**

Description: Tiny, 50' by 100', park and totlot.
Located at 12066 Semillon Boulevard, San Diego
Transit service: SDT DART   Schedules: 293-3278
Thomas Guide: Page 40, Grid F/1   Street parking
Open: 24 Hours   Jurisdiction: City of San Diego   236-6661
Restrooms: No   Picnic area: No   Public telephone: No
Walks: Area residential sidewalks only.

Serra Mesa   **Cabrillo Heights Park**

Description: Baseball and multi-purpose fields, plus a totlot.
Located at 8308 Hurlbut Street, San Diego
Transit service: SDT #16, #25   Schedules: 233-3004
Thomas Guide: Page 53, Grid D/3   On-site parking
Open: Dawn to 2200 Jurisdiction: City of San Diego   236-6661
Restrooms: Yes   Picnic tables/BBQs   Telephone: No
Walks: Try the residential area and parkways.

Serra Mesa   Murray Ridge Park

Description: Neighborhood grassed fields, playground and totlot.
Located at 8651 Celestine Avenue, San Diego
Transit service: SDT #16   Schedules: 233-3004
Thomas Guide: Page 53, Grid D/5   Parking off Escondido Ave.
Open: 24 Hours   Jurisdiction: City of San Diego   236-6661
Restrooms: No   Picnic tables: Yes   Public telephone: No
Walks: There are nice parkways and the area is walkable.

Serra Mesa   Serra Mesa Park

Description: Playgrounds, soccer, basketball and rec center.
Located at 9020 Village Glen Drive, San Diego
Transit service: SDT #16, #25   Schedules: 233-3004
Thomas Guide: Page 53, Grid E/3   Where's parking
Open: 24 Hours   Jurisdiction: City of San Diego   573-1408
Restrooms: Yes   Picnic area: Yes   Public Telephone: No
Walks: Best on parkways, and playgrounds when not in use.

Sherman Heights   Grant Hill Park

Description: Community area park with tennis courts and totlot.
Located at 2660 "J" Street, San Diego
Transit service: SDT #3, #5/105, #16   Schedules: 233-3004
Thomas Guide: Page 65, Grid E/2   On-site parking
Open: 24 Hours   Jurisdiction: City of San Diego   236-6661
Restrooms: Yes   Picnic tables: Yes   Public telephone: No
Walks: Paved parkways best. The area slopes are steep.

Sherman Heights   Sherman Little Park

Description: Neighborhood Mini-Park with totlot.
Located at 2218 Island Avenue, San Diego
Transit service: SDT #3, #5/105, #16   Schedules: 233-3004
Thomas Guide: Page 65, Grid E/2   Street parking
Open: 24 Hours   Jurisdiction: City of San Diego   236-6661
Restrooms: No   Picnic area: No   Public telephone: No
Walks: Park size is not suitable for walking.

Sorrento Valley   **Torrey Pines State Reserve**

Description: This is the inland portion of the Pines' Reserve.
Located at the end of Flintkote Avenue, San Diego
Transit service: No
Thomas Guide: Page 38, Grid C/3   Street parking
Open: Dawn to dusk   Jurisdiction: State of California   755-2063
Restrooms: No   Picnic area: No   Public telephone: No
Walks: There are 3.5 miles of random walking trails.

Spring Valley   **Goodland Acres Park**

Description: Family park, playground, horseshoes, ball court.
Located at 8825 Troy Street, Spring Valley
Transit service: CTS #856   Schedules: 233-3004
Thomas Guide: Page 62, Grid D/5   Street parking
Open: 24 Hours   Jurisdiction: County of San Diego   694-3049
Restrooms: No   Picnic area: Yes   Public telephone: No
Walks: Adjoining area is recommended. Park is 1.3 acres small.

Sunnyside   **Stephanie Rossi Memorial Trail**

Description: Sweetwater River parksite for walkers and joggers.
Located on Sweetwater Road at Briar Wood Road, Bonita
Transit service: No
Thomas Guide: Page 67, Grid C/6-D/5   On-site parking
Open: Dawn to dusk   Jurisdiction: County of S D   694-3049
Restrooms: No   Picnic area: No   Public telephone: No
Walks: The 1.5-mile loop trail explores both sides of the river.

Temecula (Riverside)   **La Serena Park**

Description: Two-block strip of grassed rolling hillside.
Located on La Serena Way and General Kearney Road.
Transit service: Greyhound bus service to Temecula.   239-9171
See a Temecula City map for location.
Open: Dawn/Dusk   Jurisdiction: Temecula City   (714) 694-6480
Restrooms: No   Picnic tables/BBQs.   Public Telephone: No
Walks: Parks slopes not suitable. Residential area is excellent.

Park Walking in San Diego County

Temecula (Riverside) Sam Hicks Monument Park

Description: Pleasant Mini-Park, playground and town museum.
Located on Mercedes Street one block North of Front Street.
Transit service: Greyhound bus service to Temecula. 239-9171
See a Temecula City map for location.
Open: Dawn/Dusk Jurisdiction: Temecula City (714) 694-6480
Restrooms: No   Picnic tables: Yes   Public Telephone: Near
Walks: A fine base from which to explore Temecula Old Town.

Temecula (Riverside) Temecula Sports Park

Description: Baseball fields and a half circle jogger's track.
Located on Margarita Road between Pauba and R'ho Vista Rds.
Transit service: Greyhound bus service to Temecula. 239-9171
See a Temecula City map for location.
Open: Dawn/Dusk Jurisdiction: Temecula City (714) 694-6488
Restrooms: Yes   Picnic area: No   Public Telephone: Yes
Walks: Jogger's track could be used when ball field not in use.

Tierrasanta Mission Trails Regional Park

Description: Largest U.S. urban park with 5740 primitive acres.
Located on both sides of Fr. Junipero Serra Trail, San Diego
Transit service: CTS #846, #847   Schedules: 233-3004
Thomas Guide: Page 54, Grid E/1   On-site parking
Open: Dawn to dusk Jurisdiction: City of San Diego 236-6582
Restrooms: Yes   Picnic area: Yes   Public telephone: No
Walking: Well known for its wide selection of nature trails.

Tierrasanta

Description: Neighborhood recreation facility with a totlot.
Located at 4734 La Cuenta Drive, San Diego
Transit service: SDT #27   Schedules: 233-3004
Thomas Guide: Page 54, Grid B/2   Street parking
Open: 24 Hours   Jurisdiction: City of San Diego   236-6661
Restrooms: No   Picnic area: No   Public telephone: No
Walks: Would be best in the nearby residential area.

Tierrasanta

Description: A wilderness canyon of many interesting aspects.
Located at 6100 Antigua Boulevard, San Diego
Transit service: No (Greenbelt Park on Santos is another entry)
Thomas Guide: Page 46, Grid B/6   Street parking
Open: 24 Hours   Jurisdiction: City of San Diego   236-6661
Restrooms: No   Picnic tables: Yes   Public telephone: No
Walks: Look for small entry sign on Antigua. A hiker's paradise.

Tierrasanta

Description: Major facility, tennis, ballfields, recreation, totlot.
Located at 11220 Clairemont Mesa Boulevard, San Diego
Transit service: No
Thomas Guide: Page 46, Grid C/6   On-site parking
Open: 24 Hours   Jurisdiction: City of San Diego   573-1394
Restrooms: Yes   Picnic tables/BBQs   Public telephone: Yes
Walking: A good variety of parkways, both paved and natural.

Tierrasanta   **Villa Monserate**

Description: Pleasant park with playground equipment, totlot.
Located at 10283 Perez Court, San Diego
Transit service: SDT #27   Schedules: 233-3004
Thomas Guide: Page 46, Grid B/6   Street parking
Open: 24 Hours   Jurisdiction: City of San Diego   236-6661
Restrooms: No   Picnic tables: Yes   Public telephone: No
Walks: Both parkways and residential area are very walkable.

University City   **Marcy Park**

Description: Modest neighborhood park, canyon view and totlot.
Located at 5504 Stresemann Street, San Diego
Transit service: SDT #5/105   Schedules: 233-3004
Thomas Guide: Page 44, Grid C/5   Street parking
Open: 24 Hours   Jurisdiction: City of San Diego   236-6661
Restrooms: No   Picnic tables: Yes   Public telephone: No
Walks: There is a loop parkway and a nice residential area.

University City   **Rose Canyon Open Space Park**

Description: 245-Acre canyon area with a wealth of hiking trails.
Located at 6950 Genesee Avenue, facing University High School
Transit service: SDT #41   Schedules: 233-3004
Thomas Guide: Page 44, Grid E/3   Limited parking
Open: 24 Hours   Jurisdiction: City of San Diego   236-6661
Restrooms: No   Picnic area: No   Public telephone: No
Walks: A walker's park with a variety of excellent trails.

University City   **Standley Park and Recreation Area**

Description: Rec center, tennis, entry to San Clemente Canyon.
Located at 3585 Governor Drive, San Diego
Transit service: SDT #5/105   Schedules: 233-3004
Thomas Guide: Page 44, Grid E/4   On-site parking
Open: 24 Hours   Jurisdiction: City of San Diego   452-8556
Restrooms: Yes   Picnic tables/BBQs   Public telephone: No
Walks: Try the parkways, canyon trails and residential area.

University City   University Gardens Park

Description: Neighborhood ballfields, playground and totlot.
Located at 6431 Gullstrand Street, San Diego
Transit service: SDT #5   Schedules: 233-3004
Thomas Guide: Page 44, Grid F/4   On-site parking
Open: 24 Hours   Jurisdiction: City of San Diego   236-6661
Restrooms: No   Picnic tables/BBQs   Public telephone: No
Walks: Use grassed parkland and adjoining small canyon.

University City   University Village Park

Description: Modest neighborhood park with view of the area.
Located at 7150 Florey Street, San Diego
Transit service: SDT #5   Schedules: 233-3004
Thomas Guide: Page 44, Grid F/3   Street parking
Open: 24 Hours   Jurisdiction: City of San Diego   236-6661
Restrooms: No   Picnic tables: Yes   Public telephone: No
Walks: On grassed fields and in adjacent residential area.

University City   Weiss-Eastgate City Park

Description: Ballcourts, pool, baseball, tennis and totlot.
Located at 4275 Eastgate Mall, San Diego
Transit service: SDT #34   Schedules: 233-3004
Thomas Guide: Page 44, Grid E/1   Street parking
Open: 24 Hours   Jurisdiction: City of San Diego   236-6661
Restrooms: No   Picnic area: No   Public telephone: No
Walks: Best in adjoining area of high-rise office buildings.

University Heights   Old Trolley Barn Park

Description: Neighborhood park with playground and totlot.
Located at 1900 Adams Avenue, San Diego
Transit service: SDT #11   Schedules: 233-3004
Thomas Guide: Page 60, Grid D/2   Street parking
Open: 24 Hours   Jurisdiction: City of San Diego   236-6661
Restrooms: No   Picnic tables: Yes   Public telephone: No
Walks: On the paved loop parkway and in the residential area.

Park Walking in San Diego County

Valley Center   Hellhole Canyon Open Space Preserve

Description: 1700 Acres, natural terrain, miles of hiking trails.
Located at 19324 Kiavo Drive and Santee Lane, Valley Center
Transit service: No.   Jurisdiction: County of San Diego
Thomas Guide: Page 12-N, Grid E/1   On-site parking weekends
Open: Auto gate open weekends.   Walkers may enter anytime
Information: 565-3600   Restrooms: No   Picnic area: No
Public Telephone: No   Walks: This is a superb primitive area

Valley Center   Robert Adams Community Park

Description: Small site, tennis, nice tree-shaded grassed areas.
Located at 28751 Cole Grade Road, Valley Center
Transit service: No.   Park open dawn to dusk
Thomas Guide: Page 12-M, Grid D/1   On-site parking
Jurisdiction: V. C. Community Service District   749-8852
Restrooms: No   Picnic area: Yes   Public Telephone: Yes.
Walks: Topography of park is not suitable for serious walking.

Vista   Breeze Hill Park

Description: Five-acre park with baseball and play fields.
Located at 900 South Melrose Drive, Vista
Transit service: NCTD # 331   Schedules: 722- or 743-6283
Thomas Guide: Page 15, Grid B/1   On-site parking
Open: Dawn to dusk   Jurisdiction: City of Vista   724-6121
Restrooms: Yes   Picnic tables/BBQs Public telephone: Yes
Walks: Area sidewalks are more suitable for walking exercise.

Park Walking in San Diego County

Vista   **Brengle Terrace Park**

Description: Superbly developed community park with sports
fields, amphitheater, recreation building and playgrounds.
Located at 1200 Vale Terrace Drive, Vista
Transit service: NCTD #331   Schedules: 722 or 743-6283
Thomas Guide: Page 11, Grid E/4   On-site parking
Open: Dawn to 2200   Jurisdiction: City of Vista   724-6121
Restrooms: Yes   Picnic tables/BBQs Public telephone: Yes
Walking: 58-Acre site has space for pleasant exercise walking.

Vista   **Bub Williamson Park**

Description: Nice neighborhood park, baseball and play fields.
Located at 530 Grapevine Lane, Vista
Transit service: NCTD # 302   Schedules: 722- or 743-6283
Thomas Guide: Page 10, Grid F/6   On-site parking
Open: Dawn to dusk   Jurisdiction: City of Vista   724-6121
Restrooms: Yes   Picnic tables/BBQs Public telephone: Yes
Walks: The surrounding residential area would be best.

Vista   **Buena Vista Park**

Description: Large multi-purpose play field, baseball and totlot.
Located at 1851 South Melrose Drive, Vista
Transit service: Vista FAST   Schedules: 940-9697
Thomas Guide: Page 15. Grid C/4   On-site parking
Open: Dawn to dusk   Jurisdiction: City of Vista   724-6121
Restrooms: Yes   Picnic tables/BBQs Public Telephone: No
Walks: Jogger's path and 43 acres when fields are not in use.

Vista   **Cedar Lane Park**

Description: Small neighborhood park with totlot.
Located at 555 Olive Avenue, Vista
Transit service: NCTD #311   Schedules: 722 or 743-6283
Thomas Guide: Page 11, Grid B/5   Street parking
Open: Dawn to dusk   Jurisdiction: City of Vista   724-6121
Restrooms: No   Picnic tables/BBQs Public telephone: No
Walks: Little room on the parksite but nearby area is walkable.

Vista   **Civic Center Park**

Description: Tennis, play field and totlot on seven acres.
Located at 600 Eucalyptus Avenue, Vista
Transit service: NCTD #331   Schedules: 722 or 743-6283
Thomas Guide: Page 11, Grid D/5   On-site parking
Open: Dawn to dusk   Jurisdiction: City of Vista   724-6121
Restrooms: Yes   Picnic tables/BBQs Public telephone: No
Walks: Parksite not suitable. Area streets are congested.

Vista   **Guajome Regional Park**

Description: A 165-acre natural park with a historic adobe
building and a farm machinery museum with rural artifacts.
Located at 2040 North Santa Fe Avenue, Vista
Transit service: NCTD #306   Schedules: 722 or 743-6283
Thomas Guide: Page 11, Grid B/2   On-site parking
Open: Call   Jurisdiction: City of Vista   941-1791
Restrooms: Yes   Picnic area: Yes   Public telephone: Yes
Walks: On Museum section. Historic adobe visits by reservation.

Vista   **Park Site**

Description: Undeveloped part of Buena Vista Park expansion.
Located at 2600 South Melrose Avenue, Vista
Transit service: Vista FAST   Schedules: 940-9697
Thomas Guide: Page 15, Grid C/5   Street parking
Open: No   Jurisdiction: City of Vista   724-6121
Restrooms: No   Picnic area: No   Public telephone: No
Walks: Undeveloped land not suitable for walking.

Vista

Park Site

Description: Undeveloped canyon for Buena Vista expansion.
Located off Jewell Ridge and Opal Ridge Streets, Vista
Transit service: Vista FAST   Schedules: 940-9697
Thomas Guide: Page 15, Grid C/5   Street parking
Open: No   Jurisdiction: City of Vista   724-6121
Restrooms: No   Picnic area: No   Public Telephone: No
Walks: Undeveloped natural land not suitable for walking.

Vista

Raintree Park

Description: A very small park with a ball court and totlot.
Located at 545 East Los Angeles Street, Vista
Transit service: Vista FAST   Schedules: 940-9607
Thomas Guide: Page 11, Grid C/4   Street parking
Open: Dawn to 2200   Jurisdiction: City of Vista   724-6121
Restrooms: No   Picnic tables: Yes   Public telephone: No
Walks: The adjoining residential area is suitable for walks.

Vista

Recreation Park

Description: Recreation building, baseball, ball court and totlot.
Located at 160 Recreation Drive, Vista
Transit service: Vista Transit Center Schedules:722 or 743-6283
Thomas Guide: Page 11, Grid C/5   Parking: Very limited.
Open: Dawn to dusk   Jurisdiction: City of Vista   724-6121
Restrooms: Yes   Picnic tables/BBQs Public telephone: Yes
Walks: No parkways and heavily congested nearby streets.

Vista

Thibodo Park

Description: Recreation building, tennis, ball court and totlot.
Located at 1150 Lupine Hills Road, Vista
Transit service: NCTD Vista FAST   Schedules: 722- or 743-6283
Thomas Guide: Page 15, Grid D/3   Limited on-site parking
Open: Dawn to 2200   Jurisdiction: City of Vista   724-6121
Restrooms: Yes   Picnic tables: Yes   Public telephone: No
Walks: There are a few park paths. Nearby area very attractive.

Vista

Description: Mini-Park with a gazebo and totlot.
Located at 615 East Vista Way, Vista
Transit service: NCTD #306   Schedules: 722 or 743-6283
Thomas Guide: Page 11, Grid D/5   Street parking
Open: Dawn to dusk   Jurisdiction: City of Vista   724-6121
Restrooms: Yes   Picnic tables/BBQs   Public telephone: No
Walks: Parksite is too small and area streets carry heavy traffic.

Index

Park Walking in San Diego County

Park Walking in San Diego County

Park Walking in San Diego County

Walks Record

Date	Where	Notes	Miles

Park Walking in San Diego County

Walks Record

Date	Where	Notes	Miles

Park Walking in San Diego County

Walks Record

Date	Where	Notes	Miles

Park Walking in San Diego County

Walks Record

Date	Where	Notes	Miles

Walks Record

Date	Where	Notes	Miles

Park Walking in San Diego County

BEACH WALKING

In San Diego County

*A complete guide to every San Diego County beach from the Orange County line
to the Mexican border. Where to park, restrooms, food services, access
streets or paths, condition of the water front, picnic facilities, best places
to walk, unique features, lifeguard services, telephone numbers and
nearby public parks or recreational facilities. (ISBN 0-910390-33-9)*

MALL WALKING

In San Diego County

*Your authoritative guidebook to more than 225 measured easy walking ventures
with descriptions of 113 San Diego malls and shopping cen-
ters. Included are details of the best public transportation,
street directions, parking lot security, restrooms, food services
and more for the suburban mall-walker. Plus separate chap-
ters on shoe selection, clothing and techniques of exercise
walking. (ISBN 0-919390-31-2)*

PARK WALKING

In San Diego County

For exercise walks or family picnics, this is the best-ever source-book for over 384
*public parks in San Diego County. Here is a park
telephone number, address, car parking locale,
source of public transportation and open hours. Use
of BBQs, picnic tables, restrooms, play areas, ath-
letic facilities, and parkways for outdoor walks is
listed. This is a most useful handbook you will enjoy
for many years to come.(ISBN 0-910390-32-0)*

Available from your local bookseller.